Not Evangelical Enough!

Not Evangelical Enough!

Edited by Iain Taylor

PATERNOSTER
PRESS

Copyright © 2003 Iain Taylor

First Published in 2003 by Paternoster Press

09 08 07 06 05 04 03   7 6 5 4 3 2 1

Paternoster Press is an imprint of Authentic Media,
PO Box 300, Carlisle, Cumbria, CA3 0QS, UK
and PO Box 1047, Waynesboro, GA 30830-2047, USA
www.paternoster-publishing.com

The right of Iain Taylor to be
identified as the Editor of this Work has been
asserted by him in accordance with
Copyright, Designs and Patents Act 1988

British Library Cataloguing in Publication Data

A catalogue record for this book is available from
the British Library

ISBN 1-84227-174-1

Cover design by FourNineZero
Printed in Great Britain by
Cox and Wyman, Reading

Contents

Introduction

Not Evangelical Enough! This ought to be a criticism that all Christians should seek to avoid. All Christians of whatever denomination should strive to be evangelical, that is, to be gospel people. Just as every Christian church and every Christian believer should seek to be catholic in the proper sense, that is, to trace the universal scope of the truth of the gospel, so they should also seek to be evangelical in the proper sense. To be evangelical, as this book will stress again and again, is to be gospel people. What it means to be evangelical is to have one's life, thought, church fellowship and theology shaped by the gospel. As the term suggests, any significant or worthy meaning of the name is to be sought in the gospel, the *evangel*, and there above all.

Not Evangelical Enough! This ought especially to be a criticism that all those who own the name 'Evangelicals' should seek strenuously to avoid. For a group of Christians who have so explicitly characterized themselves as gospel people not to have lived up to their self-identity would be a matter of serious concern. This book is intended as a challenge to this 'Evangelical' constituency, though to a wider churchmanship as well, we hope. It is not so much a critique that they have missed the mark, though at times points of criticism may be made. Rather, it is a challenge to be clear about what the mark is, what in fact it does and does not mean to be evangelical.

What often passes as 'Evangelical' on the lips of both its advocates and detractors does a disservice to what is truly evangelical. It is our conviction that when it is made clear what a truly evangelical vision consists of, and how broad, beautiful and enriching the gospel truly is, it will have its own Spirit-inspired attraction. One may feel dissatisfied with 'Evangelical' dryness, narrow-mindedness and subculture, and seek a better alternative. Maybe rightly so. This book will serve as a plea to such people not to give up on the gospel, not thereby also to give up on what is truly evangelical. There may be evil to get rid of, but there is also good to hold on to.

Not Evangelical Enough! This is a criticism that we hope those who own the name of Christ should be able to understand and avoid. To be evangelical is a work of God's grace and so is neither at our disposal nor in our control. And it is not, properly understood, a party group to belong to or a package of propositions to adopt (although, of course, the gospel will constrain us both in how we organize ourselves and in how we articulate its content). To be evangelical, at least this side of the eschaton, means a constant striving, always on the way but never definitively having arrived. The verdict of evangelical, if by that is meant conformity to God's gospel, is not one that can ultimately be decided by any human jurisdiction, by the sort of church one goes to, the books one reads or the dogmas one holds. The verdict of being evangelical in the true sense is one that ultimately only God can give, when His mortifying and vivifying grace will either commend or mock our attempts to follow the teaching and example of His Son. To be in line with the gospel, to be truly evangelical, therefore, is a goal to strive after. At any particular time the church may or may not be in line with the calling given by its Lord. But in this age the church must be aware that its orthodoxy and evangelical credentials, as much as anything else, are a constant seeking, a constant crying 'Come, Lord Jesus!', a constant questioning whether it is evangelical enough.

It is not that a critical spirit is being advocated. Far from it. If anything, we hope this will be an exercise of removing the plank from our own eye before that of removing the speck from the other's eye. Nor is it a church already made perfect that is being demanded. Rather, by getting clear again on the primacy, content and scope of the gospel itself, God's people can enjoy the freedom of a life that in all its aspects keeps in step with Christ's Spirit and expectantly awaits His return in glory. 'Evangelicals' and 'Evangelical' leaders who have settled on a fairly clear idea of what the gospel and its ministry are need not take refuge in the claim that 'there is no perfect church' any more than the seven churches of Asia Minor might have. The question to all Christ's followers is one of gospel faithfulness – whether we are evangelical enough.

Now, what is this gospel that is the test of true evangelical credentials? In its shortest form it can be the name 'Jesus Christ' or the statement 'Jesus is Lord'. A much longer form would be the collection of writings that we know as the Bible. Particularly successful attempts to summarize the gospel that are longer than the name Jesus Christ but shorter than the whole text of Scripture include the Apostles' Creed and the Nicene Creed. There are no absolute rules for how one talks about the gospel as long as its source is Scripture and its focus is Jesus Christ. And there is no absolute guarantee that any and every attempt to talk from Scripture about Jesus Christ will be the gospel, that is, will be truly evangelical. We can only speak truly of God, that is, according to His gospel, as His grace enables us. It is not something we can do on our own without Him. But since God is gracious and since He has been prepared to go to any lengths whatsoever to ensure that we do not remain on our own without Him, Christians can know and speak about the gospel, confident that God will give us thoughts and words to love Him with our minds and lips.

This book will not outline an exhaustive account of what the gospel is; far less will it offer any concise definitions of the gospel. Such definitions may tend to reduce the gospel or make unhelpful distinctions between primary and secondary issues, both of which tendencies this book will want to question. But we may say for now that the gospel is about God's Son, Jesus Christ. It is about how He chose to live not only in the eternal life of Father, Son and Holy Spirit, but also as man when, in loving obedience to the Father, He was born of the Virgin Mary and lived a life as the Jesus of Scripture. His life and work are focused on His death on the cross and His resurrection, by which He saved us from our sins and reconciled us to the Father. He has ascended to heaven and has sent us His Spirit who lives in His people and works in us all that Christ has done. He will come again one day to complete His task of salvation in resurrection and judgement, and there will be a new heaven and a new earth. This in brief and inexact outline is the gospel with which we are dealing in this book: the gospel that – we pray and hope – is also the theme of the Bible, and the gospel that is the test of what is and is not evangelical.

Two Revealing Comments

There are a couple of revealing comments made recently that are remarkable, not because of their uniqueness, but because of how common they are – they are the sort of thing I have heard again and again on the lips of 'Evangelicals'. They both have an air of plausibility, and no doubt spring from the wisdom of many years of faithful service of our Lord's gospel, but both fall short in important respects of an outlook that is evangelical in the true sense.

The first was the remark, broadcast very recently, of a leading churchman at the time of the publication of the candidly theologically liberal book *Honest to God*[1] by the then Bishop of Woolwich, John Robinson. The occasion and the date may belong only to the past, but not the remark. Responding to the bishop's confession of his doubts about traditional orthodoxy, this churchman said something to this effect. 'Your book, Bishop John, may be fitting for one such as yourself, with your high office and your great learning. But I would question whether it is wise to share such thoughts with the faithful in the pew, who might be unsettled by your thoughts. For them it is better to teach the simple milk of the gospel.'

This is a defence of the gospel, but it is surely a double-edged one. It presupposes (by no means an exception for

'Evangelicals') that the gospel has no place either in the House of Bishops or in the university theology faculty, but is the preserve of 'simple' Christians. To follow this sort of reasoning, one would have to concede that the gospel was useful for some situations but not for all, and relevant for some situations but not for all. Even worse, one might suspect that the only parts the gospel can reach are ones that have been transcended by the ecclesiologically advanced bishop and by the intellectually advanced theologian. May it not be that the gospel has been reduced to a resource only for the simpleminded and immature, and so might later prove dispensable?

The second remark was again by a leading churchman in 'Evangelical' circles at a talk made no more than ten days before my writing this introduction. Reflecting on the essentials of ministry, he said something like this:

> Keep reading your Bible, because this will sustain you throughout your Christian life. It is God's word, and if you want to find out what He has to say to you, you just have to read it. And we have to be faithful to it, too, and study it to find out what is sound and orthodox. But we need more than just orthodoxy – we need the Spirit too. Orthodoxy can be dry and dull. It can satisfy the head and all those intellectual questions you might have. There are lots of Christians who know all about the gospel and the intricacies of doctrine. They are well versed in orthodoxy. But it can't satisfy the heart and give you that life and freedom which you can only get with the Spirit.

This too, for all its emphasis on word and Spirit, has a certain ambivalence about it. If we forgive him the assumption that right and orthodox knowledge of God in the gospel is somehow less the work of the Spirit than emotional joy and desire for God, the speaker could perhaps have been more radical in his critique of this dry orthodoxy. Do not his comments assume that the gospel is relevant for the head alone and not for the heart; that the gospel is where you go when you have an intellectual difficulty; but when you have an emotional need or spiritual dryness, you need to go elsewhere? But may it not be that the dryness of that sort of Christianity was actually the symptom of it being deficiently orthodox; of it being less than the full gospel?

There is a common problem with both these remarks. That is, they restrict the scope of the gospel. The former assumes that the gospel is the meat and drink of only a few, which one may leave behind for the greater sophistication of philosophical speculation and theological doubt. The latter assumes that the gospel is the source of head-knowledge, but for invigorating life it is left wanting and one must look elsewhere. They both concede gospel truth to a reduced formulation, as something less than able either to take on the issues of our age in a relevant and coherent manner, or to satisfy the human soul thirsting for true spiritual life. But, as this book will argue, there is no need for such concessions. The Christ who gives Himself in the gospel is all sufficient. On the one hand, He is our life and the giver of the Spirit of living waters, and on the other, He is the one in whom is all wisdom and knowledge. Why go anywhere else? If we come to Him we will find not only our heart's desire but also joy and wisdom unspeakable. His gospel is our all-sufficient resource, the strong man ready and able to do battle with all the problems of the age and with all the struggles of our existence.

A Gospel without Frontiers

It is the contention of this book that the spiritual health of the church, in particular 'Evangelical' churches, will be restored again and again by its continuity with, its trust in, and its inquiry into the gospel. Against conceptions where the gospel is limited to particular spheres of life to which one has either to limit oneself or to break free under different guidance, this book will outline something of the scope of the gospel. The gospel is a gospel without frontiers. Certainly it is to be differentiated from what it is not, but it is not to be reserved for only certain issues or situations. It is the message of life and freedom for all: for rich and poor; for scholar and simple; for black and white; for all of God's world and all people and situations within it.

At times the scope of this message of life can become obscured. When groups of 'Evangelicals' have been criticized, rightly or wrongly, for being dry, irrelevant, immature or obscurantist, the sort of Christianity they have been presenting may well be guilty of the charge. When questions are raised that challenge received 'Evangelical' views or practices, it is often assumed on both sides that departure from the traditional form entails a departure from what is truly evangelical, namely the gospel itself. But however justified the charges may be against received 'Evangelicalism'; however dry, irrelevant, immature or obscurantist it may in fact be, the gospel itself can be acquitted of any such charge. 'Evangelicalism' itself may be dispensed with, but never the command to be properly evangelical, to be guided by the gospel.

In particular, it is hoped that much of what this book contains will have a special resonance with the younger generation. Many of those who have been converted to, or have grown up in, an 'Evangelical' form of Christianity, have found that for many of the issues they face there is little useful guidance on offer. Having been used to a church environment where the importance of the Bible has been repeatedly stressed, many have been surprised to meet with the displeasure of their elders for being concerned with issues that have often been less important to received 'Evangelical' tradition, but are none the less pressing and relevant.

This sense of frustration may take many forms. In terms of daily life, there may be a dissatisfaction with received ways of understanding our relationships, both romantic and platonic. Whether what has been taught successfully blends propriety and warmth, as the gospel would have us do, needs to be submitted to the evangelical test just as much as does every other question. There may also be a desire to think more creatively about how to serve God in the workplace than is often the case. How to make our discipleship relevant to all seven days of the week rather than just focused on one may require new and different thinking.

One can see this also in terms of intellectual questions. The stereotypical (and not atypical) picture of 'Evangelical' fear of theological study being the first step on the path to 'liberal' unbelief might be queried for its assuming a rather incoherent, obscurantist and weak gospel. Not just theology, but other branches of learning too, such as the sciences and the arts, may become not the valueless material of a secular worldview, but may be transformed into witnesses to the Creator's glory.

One can see this finally in terms of Christian vocation. What should an evangelical do with his or her life? The shape of Christian witness might have a shape larger than the conversion of individual souls. And may not the tasks laid on the church by its Lord also include more than what are now currently accepted as 'church' activities? Christians are right to attach spiritual significance not just to a cluster of 'Christian' meetings and responsibilities, but to the whole shape of the lives they lead in the good world God has created. And they are right not to let their lives with others be dominated by the need for 'crisis' evangelistic conversations, but to seek that full life of witness that penetrates all they do and say.

As Michael Horton has put it:

There was a tremendous sense among the Reformation's adherents that *this* world is terribly important too. To be sure, heaven is the believer's ultimate hope, but it is in *this* world where God has chosen to reveal, act, redeem and restore . . . Where are today's Bachs, Handels, Miltons, Rembrandts, Duerers, Cranachs, Herberts and Donnes? Some of them might be found working two or three jobs to put food on the table. Others have been intimidated by well-meaning but ill-informed brothers and sisters who are convinced that unless artists are producing something useful for the church (i.e., an evangelistic tract, shirt, or bumper sticker or a church bulletin), art is a waste of God's time. Once again, the 'full-time Christian ministry' thing, which the Reformers knew as 'monkery', is the criterion for determining the legitimacy of a Christian's work. Painting, singing, playing an instrument, composing, writing, directing, acting, sculpting – these activities are callings which require no evangelistic justification. All God requires of a Christian is the very best, most creative, and profound work he or she can produce.[2]

The Christian should be encouraged that there is nothing wrong with such questions if it is faithfulness to the gospel that is sought. Indeed, it is a commendable example of Christian zeal. If, however, change is sought by turning aside from the gospel, then this step is to be resisted. But if such faithfulness to the gospel does in fact require changes in Christian teaching and practice – and who can say in advance that it does not? – then Christ's followers must seek to overcome such forces of 'Evangelical' ecclesiastical conservatism and seek a more truly evangelical path.

True and False Evangelicalism

What *should* it mean to be an evangelical? I specifically ask what *should* it mean rather than what *does* it mean. The difference is neither trivial nor negligible, and will hopefully become clear in the following discussion. A gospel without frontiers requires that even those who set themselves up as its staunchest defenders must not remain immune from its gracious and purifying critique. That one is an 'Evangelical' is of itself no guarantee that one is in fact properly evangelical, that is, in line with the gospel. This confusion lies at the heart, I believe, of why, when there arise differences from a recognizable 'Evangelical' constituency, the perception is often that, whatever the rights or wrongs of the matter, it is those that own the 'Evangelical' label that have orthodoxy and soundness on their side. Or it may be that, when 'Evangelicals' have proved to be unsatisfactory in whatever way, the goal of being evangelical or even a gospel person can be disregarded too.

This should not be, and in the following paragraphs I shall outline some of the reasons why this is often the case and some suggestions for how this might be remedied. In particular, I want to examine the term 'evangelical' more closely, because the way the term is used, especially in certain English church circles, obscures some important distinctions that are necessary for the term to retain its proper gospel reference. To this end I wish to demonstrate two things. First, that evangelical is a theological and normative term that denotes conformity to the gospel. This is a use of the word that is less common than it should be, and refers to what should be the case with every Christian. Every thought, action and word by whomever it may be should be taken captive to Christ and His gospel. This is the proper goal that marks all that is truly evangelical. Second, I argue that evangelical is not – or at least not primarily – a demographic and descriptive term that denotes a particular church group with particular values and doctrines. This is the use of the word that is common when the term is used as a label for a church constituency. This is when it refers to *what happens to be the case* with a group of Christians that call themselves by the name 'Evangelical', and is used in a sociological way to denote the sort of practices and beliefs they happen to adopt at a particular time. For the most part in this introduction, though not wholly consistently, this descriptive and demographic use of the term has been as 'Evangelical', that is, with quotation marks and as a proper name with a capital 'E' to denote its distinction from the proper and primary meaning of what is evangelical, that is, without quotation marks and completely in lower case.

Of course, with the limitations of the language there is some overlap of the terms, but the key distinction must nevertheless be maintained. Being an 'Evangelical', that is, a part of a group that adopts the name, is of itself no guarantee whatsoever that one is in fact evangelical, that is, a disciple of Christ's gospel. When this distinction becomes blurred there is the danger that people might assume they are in line with the gospel, since the group they belong to with its beliefs and practices owns the name, whereas in fact what is truly evangelical is something quite different. There is the danger of self-defensive party spirit. Furthermore, there is the danger that a rejection of much of what 'Evangelicals' happen to do means abandoning what is truly evangelical as well, rather than rebuking the constituency for praising God's gospel with their lips when their hearts are far from it. There is the danger that even the most justified frustration might automatically become a failure to search again the source of life-giving spiritual life in the true biblical gospel. In short, it is imperative to notice that evangelical is a theological term rather than a demographic one, and to treat it that way.

I hope that what I have said is clear, but I shall clarify further this essential distinction, which is not so easy to express in the English language. The two German words for our 'evangelical' are *evangelisch* and *evangelikal*. For our purposes we can appropriate them in this way: *evangelisch* is the common adjective for the Protestantism that springs from the magisterial Reformation (that is, of Martin Luther, John Calvin, Ulrich Zwingli and Thomas Cranmer); *evangelikal* is the common adjective for a particular constituency within Protestantism that springs from the revivals of the eighteenth century.

The former term, *evangelisch*, denotes a basic decision to have one's life, one's entire thought, action, speech, church life and society, determined by and responsible to the good news of Jesus Christ. For the Reformers this stance was directed against the abuses of late-Medieval piety. The gospel was to be the final arbiter in matters of authority: the formulae of popes and councils could not be granted primary or immediate authority, but like all else these were both to be subjected to the norm of the Bible; nor could the unwritten traditions of the church function as an equal authority to God's written word of Scripture, but gospel people were to be guided by Scripture alone (*sola scriptura*). The gospel was to be the final arbiter in matters of salvation: the schema of salvation and the associated order of the sacraments, not to mention the doctrine of purgatory and the use of relics, were to be abandoned in the face of the gospel assertion of the all-sufficiency of God's gracious gift of life to us in the death of His Son Jesus Christ (*sola gratia*). This was the basic insight that, in their eyes, differentiated their positions from that of much what commonly passed for Christianity around them.

The latter term, *evangelikal*, refers to a specific group of Christians arising from the eighteenth-century revivals in English-speaking churches. These revivals and their associated piety led to the formation of various denominations, missions movements, socio-political campaigns and what is sometimes called 'the Evangelical movement'. It is true that the dominant concern of this movement was to be evangelical in the proper sense, that is, to be *evangelisch*, but in so far as this group is denoted as *evangelikal* or evangelical as a sociological and descriptive term, it does not have the same binding force as the normatively theological *evangelisch*. It is this latter term, *evangelikal*, that denotes the way the term 'Evangelical' is most often used in church circles in Great Britain, such as in the Evangelical Alliance. This constituency is the one that is the subject, for instance, of the 1989 study by David Bebbington entitled *Evangelicalism in Modern Britain: A History from the 1730s to the 1980s*[3] which outlines the four evangelical distinctives of conversionism, activism, biblicism and crucicentrism.

The point here is that many of the perceived problems with Evangelicalism may be only with the *evangelikal* notion of Evangelicalism, in which case it may not be the gospel that is under threat. If it is rather the case that the *evangelisch* notion of evangelicalism is under threat, such moves should be resisted. It is the *evangelisch* notion that must be primary; the *evangelikal* notion is dispensable. To be evangelical, if it is to be worthy of the name, must be a theological position that is wholly determined by the gospel. It cannot be a label at the command either of the church activist, sociologist or the in-crowd, but must be the verdict at God's command to be given wherever He finds conformity to His message about Jesus Christ.

With this distinction in mind, we hope that all that is good about the gospel meaning of the term evangelical will be retained. Secondary notions, however, with all their demographic dress and suspicions of party spirit, can be maintained or dispensed with depending on their correspondence to the gospel they seek to follow. Not all Evangelicalisms are the same, therefore. There is a proper, true one, which all

Christians should strive after, and there may be false ones, which, despite the name, fall short of being evangelical enough.

To paraphrase loosely some fine words of one of the most truly evangelical thinkers of the previous century:

> The reproduction of an 'Evangelical orthodoxy' is a necessary, rewarding and instructive exercise within the sphere of ecclesiastical or dogmatic history. But we cannot substitute it for, or confuse it with, the task of presenting Christian doctrine. Nor can doctrine be presented in the form of a reproduction of 'Evangelicalism'. Consultation of the Bible must mean something more than simply giving a supplementary proof – side by side with the consultation of reason – that the doctrine of the Bible is identical with that of an 'evangelical' orthodoxy . . . It is to Scripture that we must again address ourselves, not refusing to learn from it but never as part of an 'Evangelicalism without reserve'.[4]

Redefining Heterodoxy: Reductionism and Distortionism

Giving labels is often rightly frowned on, since in a false and rigid form they misrepresent the other and are self-justifying in a way that distorts the truth. That is not what is intended here. But if one wants rightly to discern the word of truth, one must guard against what deflects the believer from living in line with the gospel.

The most common labels that one gleans from much 'Evangelicalism' often do not do justice to the concerns of being truly evangelical. Rather than being defined by the contours of the gospel, they typically describe sociological or demographic features of a particular group of Christians. Perhaps the most common, the distinction between 'charismatic' and 'conservative' evangelicals, often (but not always) seems to lack real theological bite. The sociological analysis that undergirds such distinctions may help companies to know what song book brochures or book lists to send to the churches within their catchment area, but the important matters of substance are passed by. Sometimes (but again not always by any means) material differences in the respective doctrines of Scripture or the Holy Spirit are denoted. For the most part, however, the material and important questions are left unasked – What should I be, charismatic or conservative? Or both? Or neither?

There is a place for such demographic distinctions, and what is offered here is not offered as a replacement but as a complement. What is needed is a different sort of classification: one that better suits the theological centre of what is truly evangelical; one that is fitting to gospel content, not demographic dress. Others may offer more detailed and accurate formulations, but here I shall outline two syndromes to avoid where the gospel content comes under threat. I have called these false trails away from what is properly evangelical *distortionism* and *reductionism*, that is, when the gospel becomes either distorted or reduced.

Certainly this classification has obvious advantages over the almost ubiquitous conservative/charismatic one. The terms 'distortionism' and 'reductionism' follow the contours of the gospel, not the demographic phenomena of church constituencies or worship styles. They can take evangelical positions seriously and fairly, since they need not pillory either 'charismatics' as being necessarily experientialists or 'conservatives' as necessarily dry. They can serve as a guide to right and wrong, since what distorts or reduces the gospel is by definition wrong. They understand the term evangelical to be an eschatological goal all Christians should aim towards, rather than either a sociological group or constituency or a package of traditional doctrinal formulae, which may help get rid of some needless divisions while sharpening the focus on the important ones. There may be certain 'conservatives' and certain 'charismatics', for instance, who perpetually fail the test of gospel orthodoxy, but the example of the far greater number of the scrupulously faithful among both 'conservatives' and 'charismatics' is ample evidence that this is not because they belong either to the 'conservative' or 'charismatic' constituencies. For the purposes of this book, the terms distortionism and reductionism serve a particularly useful function. In the following pages we shall be exploring some of what, as Paul says, it means for 'all the treasure of wisdom and knowledge to be hidden in Jesus Christ' (Colossians 2:3). He is the one from whom, in whom and for whom are all things, and who has reconciled all things to God. All things are therefore to be understood in relation to Him. Where this does not happen, it is either because we understand Christ wrongly and thereby mistake the proper meaning of all reality, which is distortion; or it is because we understand Christ as the centre of not all, but only of some, of reality, which is reduction.

No doubt this sort of distortion and reduction is something the most well meaning of Christ's followers fall into, this book included. It is another matter, however, when these shortcomings become institutionalized to the point of being syndromes. When such is the case, distortion and reduction become distortionism and reductionism, and to speak against these is wholly justified, not hypercritical nit-picking. The goal has ceased to be truly evangelical, namely conformity to the content and scope of the gospel.

Distortionism arises when Christians exhibit a chronic failure to respect the *content* of the gospel. This may happen when the tireless, and in some senses justified, search for meaning and fulfilment leads to another source other than Jesus Christ. For instance, the authority of Scripture, which is the Spirit-filled voice of Christ to His church, becomes not the judge of inspiring ideas, but replaced by the most inspiring ideology of the age. The life-giving commands of our Lord become the poor relation of what is judged emotionally and psychologically meaningful on other criteria, and the word of salvation of Christ's atoning death and resurrection becomes smothered by a message of personal liberation that is less scandalous and less demanding. So, if it is *the gospel* that is for all life, then there will be an inevitable pastoral fall-out when the panorama of human existence is directed by an alien message.

Reductionism arises when Christians exhibit a chronic failure to respect the *scope* of the gospel. This may happen when part of the fullness of the biblical witness is deemed essential and primary and other parts are relegated to the status of being dispensable and secondary. For instance, Christ's commission to be His witnesses becomes a one-sided preoccupation with 'soul winning'; the rich variety of the life of love we are called to as Jesus' disciples becomes a limited 'Evangelical' moral code of individual morality; or the God-given task of giving to the poor and speaking in the political arena for social justice becomes a one-sided middle-class preoccupation with the 'family values' of a bygone era. So, if the gospel is for *all life*, then its limitation to only a part will inevitably have a pastoral fall-out when the rest of existence is denied the gospel's life-giving power.

When there is distortionism or reductionism there has been a basic failure to be evangelical enough. A faulty vision blurs the true nature of the gospel, which threatens either its purity or its scope, and to apply the adjective 'Evangelical' in these circumstances is to treat it as a label and to empty it of its gospel substance. Only by being evangelical in the proper sense, by a radical and thoroughgoing commitment to the full gospel of Christ, will these dangers be avoided.

An Agenda and a Proposal

This book aims to do two things. First, it seeks to make clear what it means to be evangelical, and to distinguish this from false notions, especially when they reside in the most august bastions of an 'Evangelical' orthodoxy. Second, it seeks to trace something of the full scope of the gospel. The range of the articles in the main part of the book reflects this. All the topics addressed are genuine gospel concerns. Although not every gospel concern is discussed by any means, there is enough of a spectrum of topics to illustrate that the message of Jesus Christ is indeed relevant not to part of reality, but to it all.

Issues such as social justice *and* evangelism, preaching *and* engagement with culture, and gender issues *and* the doctrine of Scripture are all treated as essential elements of the gospel that need to be considered in a rigorously evangelical way.

Martin Davie's article 'Evangelicals and their Heritage' begins the collection. There are certain accounts of the history of Evangelicalism that see the 'Evangelicals' as the good guys, as the remnant people, the true elect of God's church, who are the bastion of purity in a corrupt world and an apostate church. So the story goes, the baton of 'Evangelical' soundness of the few of earlier ages is passed on to the few of our era who, unlike so many others, hold to the same concerns and practices of the apostolic age. As a church historian with a wide knowledge of the Evangelical movement, Davie shows that such accounts are misleading.

As Davie makes clear, there is not one heritage of Evangelicalism that is absolutely pure, sound and true. Rather, it would be more accurate to say that Evangelicalism has several, indeed many, heritages. He writes:

> The impression is sometimes given that the diversity of contemporary Evangelicalism is a modern phenomenon that is the result of a decline from some previous golden age when all Evangelicals were in agreement about what Evangelicalism stood for. This impression is completely misleading. There never has been a period throughout Evangelical history from the eighteenth century onwards in which there has not been disagreement and disunity among Evangelicals.

The heritage of Evangelicalism is not simple and agreed, rather 'it is complex, pluriform and disputed'.

But not only is the attempt to trace the line of 'Evangelical' purity a rather naïve attempt to find a pot of gold at the end of the rainbow, it is also in an important sense to have missed the point. What is admirable about 'Evangelicals' of previous generations and also what goes to explain their pluriformity is that they represent related but different attempts to live in the light of the biblical gospel, that is, to use the language of this book's introduction, to be properly evangelical. And it is our conformity to this gospel of Jesus Christ, not our conformity to a revered 'Evangelical' heritage, that really matters. As Davie writes:

> The first question that has to be asked of the heritages of Evangelicalism is therefore the radical question: to what extent do they bear witness to this evangelical message of God's free grace and enable women and men to respond to it in thankful obedience.

There then follow two essays on issues that relate to the evangelical Christian's involvement in the world around him or her. Both represent a challenge to the sort of 'Evangelical' spirituality that only engages with the world to seek to convert it. As both essays argue powerfully, the gospel demands that we serve God in the world in a more comprehensive way, and that we renounce attitudes to the world around us that are not evangelical enough.

In the first essay Andy Hartropp takes up the important topic of 'Evangelicals and Social Justice'. Taking us through the biblical evidence, Hartropp demonstrates that social justice is not a peripheral issue for the Bible-believing Christian, but is a central gospel concern. The full sweep of God's action for us in creation, reconciliation and consummation shows this to be so. Following the evangelical logic of the broad scope of the gospel, Hartropp also outlines something of how this element of the Christian message will help fashion us further into the likeness of Christ. The way we work, the way we shop, the way we act towards each other at church, the way we vote and the way we engage with society are all to be affected by God's act and message of justice in Jesus Christ. He writes:

> For decades, Evangelicals in the UK have, by and large, given little attention to the Bible's teaching on social justice and injustice. Our thinking about these matters, therefore, is likely at present to be dominated by secular and unbiblical ideas. There is much renewing of our minds to be done.

The six implications that Hartropp draws from this central gospel concern should help our thinking to be renewed in relevant and faithful ways.

The next essay, 'Evangelicals and Contemporary Culture', is a plea for the right sort of evangelical worldliness, where it is the gospel that sets the agenda, as well as a critique of the wrong sort of worldliness 'Evangelicals' can be wont to fall into. Luke Bretherton argues against many common presuppositions that militate against a properly evangelical view. At one point he concludes:

> The sociologically defined influence or otherwise of Evangelicalism on contemporary culture can tell us next to nothing about the worth or righteousness of the relationship between Evangelicalism and contemporary culture. The worth of this relationship can only be evaluated by discerning the degree to which Evangelicalism constitutes a faithful witness to the life, death and resurrection of Jesus Christ, and how far its relationship with its friends, enemies and indifferent neighbours in the contemporary culture promotes or detracts from such witness.

He goes on to outline what a more gospel-centred attitude to culture would look like. In particular it means a healing of the common rift between Evangelicals' belief and practice. He explores how what the Bible has to say about both hospitality and holiness can help us relate to society around us in a way that better reflects the world that God has made and is in the process of restoring from the tragedy of human sin. Our neighbours, our society and the world around us with its diverse cultures are not to be seen as autonomous spheres that Christians must either fight against or assimilate themselves into. We can only understand them and act obediently towards them when we realize that they, no less than we, are determined by the gospel of Jesus Christ.

Then there are two pieces on what in theological circles would be called evangelical anthropology, that is, what the gospel has to say about what it means to be a human being.

That flourishing human existence and experience is a genuine concern of a rigorously biblical faith, rather than the sole preserve of its less biblical but seemingly more comfortable rivals, is clear from what David Jackman has written on 'Evangelicals and the Human Person'.

Taking us through much of the biblical material, Jackman is concerned lest the real humanity of its message be distorted into something less than human. If the relationships fostered in 'Evangelical' churches, both with those inside the community and those outside, fail to provide something of that spiritual and existential satisfaction Christ came to bring, may it be because there is a less than evangelical understanding of how God has made us and what He has done for us in Jesus Christ? Jackman is wary of the 'sort of mechanistic reductionism that is a travesty of full-orbed New Testament Christianity. This lies behind our slide into legalism and activism as well as the comparatively low expectations of growth in Christlikeness that beset contemporary "Evangelicalism".'

The gospel in its wholeness is good news for humanity in its wholeness. One should reduce neither. As Jackman puts it, in moving words:

> Jesus knows all about our human struggles – from the inside. But empathy is not His greatest gift. Rather it is His unfailing application of divine truth to all the changing scenes of life that provides such a masterclass in what it is to be a truly human being and such an example of godly living for us to follow.

The next essay tackles an issue whose importance is evident in the fact that it is as trendy a topic in the wider world as it is controversial within 'Evangelical' churches. Kristin Aune in 'Evangelicals and Gender' argues for what has been called the 'egalitarian' position on biblical manhood and womanhood. And she does so, not on the basis of some political programme and philosophy, but seeking to allow the gospel to transform our context.

For Aune, it is not what society considers acceptable that should set the terms of debate, but the witness of Scripture. She writes:

I have encountered people who justify women's leadership of churches on the grounds that 'In this day and age you can't say women can't be leaders.' While this is a line of argument that Christians may legitimately put forward after they have engaged with Scripture and asked hard questions about its interpretation, it is not a legitimate position if it is argued *without* biblical reflection, and if Western cultural ideologies are held up as supremely authoritative.

Aune is adamant that an evangelical approach to this issue should not be undermined either by the sort of selective literalism that would fall into a less than evangelical reductionism or by a naïve or unwitting conservatism that reads texts with the spectacles of a particular status quo, whether it is one side of the 1960s or the other, rather than the spectacles of the biblical gospel.

Here is a topic where the rival standpoints do often talk past one another, or take refuge in arguments that often are neither very convincing nor very central to the evangelical Christian, and it is to be hoped that those who debate with Aune either in agreement or disagreement will seek, with her, to let their points follow the gospel. It has to be said to many on both sides, 'complementarian' and 'egalitarian' alike, that no amount of comparative word studies and no amount of sociological and cultural analysis, either on their own or together, will ever provide a properly evangelical answer to this issue of gender. They can only have their force when seen in the light of that far more important – and, indeed, truly evangelical – question: 'What has happened in Jesus Christ?'

The final three essays deal with territory that one may more readily associate with the term evangelical, namely Scripture, preaching and evangelism. These three areas are ones in which 'Evangelicals' have – rightly – invested heavily, especially when other branches of the wider church may have let themselves be deflected from the absolute necessity of a biblical Christianity. To those, however, who may have thought that the gospel would have a chastening word for 'Evangelicals' only on the subjects treated so far and not on the 'safe' home territory of the last three chapters, some of the points made might prove rather uncomfortable.

In the first of these three articles, 'Evangelicals and the Bible', Paul Blackham argues that for many, including many 'Evangelicals', *sola scriptura*, or the doctrine of the sufficiency of Scripture, has been a long-forgotten principle. He unearths some of the treasures of a thoroughly evangelical treatment of Scripture by taking us through what Luther and Calvin had to say on the matter.

Blackham is eager in no way to locate Scripture's authority, that is the self-authenticating witness to Jesus Christ, in anything other than the Spirit of the Scriptures. It is His illumination that is needed more than anything else, indeed rather than anything else, if we are ever to grasp its clear and sufficient meaning. Commenting on the Barth–Harnack correspondence of the 1920s, Blackham writes:

> Understanding the Bible is a work of the Holy Spirit and cannot be achieved through any human abilities or methods. Only faith as a gift of God can show us the real Jesus. All that historical criticism can show us is that the real Jesus is impossible to know on historical–critical grounds.

It is worth noting that several shibboleths of many who would consider themselves thoroughly biblical Christians come in for rather severe examination, with some of them failing to pass the test of a truly evangelical doctrine of Scripture that is in line with the Reformers. For Blackham, apologetics does not make the grade, since it is incompatible with *sola scriptura*. Also inadequate are certain uses and understandings of Scripture's inerrancy. And as for historical criticism, this is considered a 'danger' that might lead to a 'deadly heresy' that denies the true force of this doctrine that the Reformers fought for so much, just as the modern thought of the Enlightenment has fought against it. Blackham's reading of evangelical thinkers of the past raises the searching question: are 'Evangelicals', even 'Evangelical' theologians, biblical enough?

In 'Evangelicals and Preaching' I examine how what you preach and the way you preach are necessarily affected by what you think of the content and scope of the gospel. Like the article on the Bible, this one too seeks to investigate word ministry with the strong conviction of the sufficiency of the biblical gospel and the free power of the Holy Spirit.

With three theses I outline something of what that might mean. One of the things I argue against is the tendency to see preaching as a technique. Ultimately, preachers are subject to that most excruciating embarrassment of all: that they expect, and are expected by others, to do the one thing it is impossible for them to do – that is, to impart knowledge of God where there is ignorance; divine righteousness where there is evil; and life where there is sin and death. It is the work of the Holy Spirit that is required. Impressive presentations on the part of the expert pulpit technician with knowledge and communication skills can perhaps hide the deficit that only the Spirit can make good, but they cannot get rid of it. Nor can all the workshops on preaching technique. Preaching is not a technique: it is a spiritual discipline, and therefore also a work of pure spiritual grace.

Another constant emphasis is that the preacher's sole theme is Jesus Christ. God has nothing else to say, so why should His messengers? As I put it:

> Whatever you think the Bible is talking about, if it does not find its central significance in Jesus Christ, then your reading is at odds with gospel reality. The Bible contains many words, but its heart and focus, without which all those other words are without meaning or life, is the one Word and name 'Jesus Christ'.

If God's Word is indeed powerful and sufficient, as a truly evangelical faith requires, then gospel preachers need only have this unique focus.

In the final piece in the collection, 'Evangelicals and Evangelism', Paul Weston develops a thought-provoking, theologically informed, and above all immensely practical

proposal for sharing the gospel in an effective and evangelical
way. Many will benefit on an immediate day-to-day level from
the approach outlined here, but there are also some key points
at which the gospel reality has pointed out where other strategies have been bound to less than evangelical assumptions.
For instance, in questioning the notion of 'pre-evangelism',
Weston writes:

> Jesus *starts* . . . with a gospel announcement and works through
> its implications in all that follows. It is interesting that our
> contemporary strategies have tended to reverse this process,
> starting with various 'bridging' or preparatory strategies
> designed to lead towards such an announcement.

Weston's approach would help prevent the entry into our
evangelism of the distortionism and reductionism discussed
earlier. By referring again and again to Jesus as the one who
bears witness to Himself in our evangelism, we are less likely
consistently to distort what He has to say about Himself since
we take our cue from His words and nobody else's. We are less
likely consistently to reduce the message because we will necessarily rely less on the sort of formulae and catchphrases that
obscure the immediacy and directness of Jesus' words.

The Wider 'Evangelical' World

To round off this introduction I shall consider how what has
been said here might fit into the Evangelical landscape. Much
has been written and said over recent decades on both sides of
the Atlantic about what it means to be evangelical and what
future, if any, an evangelical movement or theology might
have. So let me offer three reasons why this collection can offer
a useful and distinctive contribution to this debate.

First, this book, unlike many other works on
Evangelicalism, is not all that bothered about an 'Evangelical'
constituency as such. There are many who would not wish to
be called 'Evangelicals' who nevertheless share the gospel

concerns that mark what is evangelical in the true sense. And there are many who are zealous that their affiliation, church and lifestyle conform to a rigorously 'Evangelical' model whose isolation from genuine gospel reality means that they are not worthy of the name. What is meant here by evangelical is the same as what is meant by Christian. Whatever one's tradition, any disciple of Christ is to be governed by and judged by the good news of Jesus Christ. All Christians, then, are or should be, to a greater or lesser extent, evangelical in the true sense. It is a book, therefore, that is thoroughly ecumenical in intention.

Second, this book hopes to provide a framework so that Christian leaders and churches can work out for themselves what is in line with the gospel, that is, what is truly evangelical. In particular, by shifting attention away from false notions of 'Evangelical' as a package offered by a specific church subculture to true notions of fidelity to a gospel that is not the property or at the disposal of any group, one can resolve some debates where positions have become entrenched. The old guard need not think that to be evangelical they have to defend the formulations and techniques of a previous generation and need not identify their own understanding of gospel truth with that truth itself. The new guard need not think that in criticizing or changing the received norms of an 'Evangelical' establishment or heritage they can also dispense with true evangelical gospel reality.

For instance, Dave Tomlinson's stimulating book *The Post-evangelical*[5] can be seen as a perceptive critique of the wrong sort of 'Evangelical' Christianity. In this book, of course, we have taken a quite different approach from Tomlinson, since we believe that the name evangelical is worth maintaining and defending. He believes that it is the cultural situation of post-modernity that demands a different sort of Christianity from the Evangelicalism of modernity, and to this we must answer that this is not a sufficient reason. A new cultural situation can entail only at best a different presentation of the gospel message, not a change in the content itself. Yet such a change in content may indeed be called for if the 'Evangelical' presentation of the gospel falls short of the right evangelical content, and here some of Tomlinson's critiques may have something important to say.

It might be that some of the perceptive critiques of the Evangelicalism Tomlinson is used to can be better shaped and resolved when seen as pleas from pastoral experience for the full relevance of the gospel to be set free from the strictures many 'Evangelicals' have laid on it.

For instance, the sorts of ideas in the essays here on 'Evangelicals and Contemporary Culture' and 'Evangelicals and Social Justice' might be the basis for an evangelical understanding of the Christian 'worldliness' he advocates.[6] 'Evangelicals' may or may not be obscurantist, narrow-minded and unappreciative of all the creative beauty of culture, but there is no need for a true evangelical outlook to follow this path. 'Evangelicals' may busy themselves with enough church activities and Christianized subculture to fill the time they perhaps should have spent getting involved in this fallen world God has created and reconciled to Himself, but not true gospel people.

I wonder whether Tomlinson's critique of 'Evangelicals' treating human beings as things with brains rather than as persons with wills, affections and feelings can be more forcefully put, not as being somehow outdated by cultural shifts, but as the symptom of an insufficiently evangelical understanding of the personhood.[7] He may not agree wholly, but he might be pleasantly surprised with some of the things written in the piece on 'Evangelicals and the Human Person', particularly if he were to learn that this has been written by the director of the Cornhill Training Course!

Third, this book can help foster a greater sense of the whole of the gospel. There are pressures to restrict the gospel of Jesus Christ to only part of life in this world. There are some Christians who want to talk about issues in the world and think the gospel of Jesus is not very relevant to them. And there are some who want to talk about the gospel of Jesus, but it is a gospel that is in danger of losing some of its relevance to the world.

There is, for instance, a common reading of recent 'Evangelical' history in Great Britain that goes against the grain of our argument so far. It runs something like this. In the first half of the century, Bible-believing 'Evangelicals' were a faithful but isolated minority. Against an establishment of liberals and high churchmen, 'Evangelicals' confined themselves to small-scale evangelism and to Free churches. Since the war, however, Evangelicalism has gained not only a popular following but greater respectability in both the academy and the wider church. Now the 'Evangelical' constituency of churchgoers is rising, if not in overall numbers, then at least as a percentage of church life.

This 'Evangelical' renaissance has had several important leaders, such as Billy Graham and J.I. Packer. But probably the most important leader in Britain has been John Stott. Stott, in his ministries at All Souls, Langham Place, London, and in the rest of the world, has overseen the growth of the sort of Evangelicalism that was a minority concern in his youth into a mainstream part of established church life. While immensely grateful for and complimentary of Stott's leadership, there have been two question marks raised concerning his legacy.

The first is his relations with the wider church, in particular his insistence at Keele[8] that Evangelicals should work within their own denominations. Some have thought that certain subsequent developments, such as the ordination of women, the apparent lack of sound 'Evangelical' orthodoxy in the Anglican House of Bishops, even the holder of the Archbishopric of Canterbury, are reasons for a moratorium on close involvement in the denomination until it has undergone some necessary reform. The rights and wrongs of such issues, where the rhetoric of true and false Evangelicalism is particularly acute, need not concern us here.

The second has to do with the scope of Stott's writing ministry in recent years. Since the late 1970s Stott has published substantial works both on the atonement and on socio-political involvement. According to the interpretation we are investigating here, there is a certain ambivalence to this twin focus. On the one hand, the work on the atonement, *The Cross of Christ*,[9] is, so they say, a magnificent statement of evangelical belief. On the other hand, the works on social involvement, *Contemporary Issues Facing Christians Today* and *The Contemporary Christian*,[10] for all the good lessons in their pages, leave the door open to a sort of social gospel that is threatening to become prevalent again and to take us back to the sort of liberal establishment of the pre-war years. According to this reading, the fear is that Stott's legacy will be the latter books, not the former, and that as a result Evangelicalism will lose sight of its gospel centre.

The danger with such readings, notwithstanding the perhaps too swift identification of gospel truth with the traditions of a particular 'Evangelical' group, is that they encourage a reduction of the gospel. The point is taken that it would be wrong to follow those of an earlier age for whom the Christian life meant involvement in political causes and not evangelism, or that social concern is what Christianity is all about and that biblical preaching is dispensable. But one still goes seriously wrong if one maintains the dichotomy between evangelism and care for the needy and promotes a model of church life and 'Evangelical' spirituality that reinforces it. Even where it is acknowledged that the gospel might have something to say about social issues, it is common for this to be a merely theoretical acknowledgement and not a practical one. Social action is often relegated to the interest of parachurch organizations and is not considered important for the life of the local church. It is not given serious thought by church leaders; it is not integrated into the life of the church community; it is not considered to be part of Christian discipleship. Immense time and effort can be taken up with a host of evangelistic dinner parties, but none at all with a soup kitchen. To all intents and purposes, care for the needy can become an 'optional' component of the Christian life.

Yet such attitudes and practices will not do. To think and act in these terms is just to accept the false dichotomy that the old 'social gospel' movement maintained between evangelism and preaching on the one hand and social concern on the other. All that is different is that one side of the dichotomy is chosen rather than the other.

It is of course correct that works such as *The Cross of Christ* do indeed deal with matters of central importance for gospel people. Jesus did not choose any other destiny for Himself, nor will the apostle boast in anything else. But biblical faithfulness cannot stop there. Did not Amos preach a social gospel? Did not Isaiah? Did not James? Did not Paul? And did not Jesus? Who knows? Maybe God's Word to us now – like Jesus' message to the Pharisees of the first century – is that there should be a bit less legalistic orthodoxy and Bible study and a bit more compassion and care for the poor. But then we need not choose between scriptural faithfulness and care for the poor. On this matter the gospel is not either–or, it is both–and. Scripture's witness to Jesus Christ commands us to care for both our neighbour's soul and body; both to tell others about Jesus' death for us and to defend the cause of the oppressed; both to lead others to deeper knowledge of biblical truth, and to advocate greater justice in all we do in our lives. And it is this both–and that Stott has so rightly recognized and so clearly articulated against certain tendencies 'Evangelicals' (like their liberal 'social gospel' brothers and sisters) may have had in the past to separate what God has joined. He has not let himself be bound by this unevangelical dichotomy and has – seeking to follow the biblical gospel – thought about, written about and emphasized both. Indeed, whether one agrees or disagrees with him at any or every point, one of the great legacies of John Stott has been his grasp on the scope of the gospel and his explaining it in all its rich fullness.

For all the apparent 'Evangelical' soundness of fearing the dilution of the gospel by foreign elements, these sorts of arguments can only succeed if the elements that cause alarm are indeed foreign to the gospel. And one must be on guard here lest the gospel one is defending is not a true version, but a reduced one. The defender of a reduced gospel will inevitably consider some things that really do belong to the heart of the gospel to be alien elements that have to be resisted. But to do this – no less than the distortionism that accepts as gospel reality what really is alien to it – would be a failure to be evangelical enough.

Notes

1 John Robinson, *Honest to God* (London: SCM, 1963).
2 Michael Horton, *Putting Amazing Back into Grace* (London: Hodder & Stoughton 1994), p. 252.
3 David Bebbington, *Evangelicalism in Modern Britain: A History from the 1730s to the 1980s* (London and New York: Routledge, 1989).
4 This is a paraphrase of a critique of certain Calvinists in K. Barth *Church Dogmatics* 2.2 (Edinburgh: T&T Clark, 1956), p. 36.
5 D. Tomlinson, *The Post-evangelical* (London: Triangle, 1995).
6 Ibid. p. 125. In the chapter 'Positively Worldly' Tomlinson writes: 'Few topics are more important to post-evangelicals than the Christian's relationship with the world. The "parallel universe" of alternativism [that is, cutting oneself off from the world to form a Christian sub-culture or ghetto] constitutes a substantial part of what they wish to leave behind.'
7 Ibid. pp. 125–6. Tomlinson writes on the postmodern and post-evangelical situation:

It is a world in which people now reject truth claims which are expressed in the form of dogma or absolutes. It is a world in which dignity is granted to emotions and intuition, and where people are accustomed to communicating through words linked to images and symbols rather than through plain words or simple statements. It is a world in which people have come to feel a close affinity with the environment, and where there is a strong sense of global unity. It is a world in which people are deeply suspicious of institutions, bureaucracies and hierarchies. And perhaps most importantly of all, it is a world in which the spiritual dimension is once again talked about with great ease. Post-evangelical people, I think, are people who belong to, or are influenced by, this world, and whose Christian faith is increasingly being expressed in and through this frame of reference.

8 The first National Evangelical Anglican Congress met at Keele University in 1967.
9 John Stott, *The Cross of Christ* (Leicester: IVP, 1986).
10 John Stott, *Contemporary Issues Facing Christians Today* (Leicester: IVP, 1983) and John Stott, *The Contemporary Christian* (Leicester: IVP, 1990).

1

Evangelicals and their Heritage

Martin Davie

Introduction

Some years ago I came across an Independent Evangelical Chapel that claimed on its notice board that it was 'founded in AD 33'. As a sceptical church historian, I was dubious about this claim, especially as the church building suggested a more accurate date of around 1933CE.

However, although in one sense the claim made by that particular chapel was historically absurd, nevertheless in another sense the claim was true. Indeed, it could even be argued that the date suggested was too late rather than too early. The reason I say this is that, if one traced the history of that chapel back in time, what one would find would be an unbroken chain of historical succession that would link its history via the English Reformation to the history of the medieval and patristic church, and behind that to the church of the Apostolic era, and further back still to the history of Israel beginning with the call of Abraham in the early second millennium BCE.

What this means is that if we ask about the heritage to which that chapel was the heir we are dealing with a very

large subject indeed. It is the heir to all the previous history
to which I have just referred and all this history will continue to affect its life today.

The point I have just made about the history of that particular
chapel would also be true for all other Evangelical churches,
chapels and movements. They are all heirs to a complex historical heritage that continues to shape their particular version of
Evangelical Christianity. In this paper I want to explore in more
detail the various strands that go to make up this Evangelical
heritage and to suggest how we should respond to that heritage
in a theologically responsible fashion.

1. What is an Evangelical?

Before I can begin this main task, however, I need first of all to
explain what I mean when I use the term 'Evangelical', since
this is a term that has been used in three distinct ways.

First, in the sixteenth century, it was used as a general term
to describe supporters of the Protestant Reformation, and its
German equivalent *evangelisch* is still used in this way today.
Thus the established Protestant church in Germany, which is a
union of Lutheran, Reformed and United Churches, is the
Evangelische Kirche in Deutschland (EKD).

Second, *evangelisch* also came to be used to refer to Protestants
who were Lutheran rather than Reformed in persuasion.
Because of this secondary German usage, the term Evangelical is
used as a label by contemporary American Lutherans. Thus
the largest Lutheran denomination in the United States is the
Evangelical Lutheran Church in America (ELCA).

Now, neither the EKD nor the ELCA would necessarily be
seen as Evangelical churches by most people in this country
who would describe themselves as Evangelical. This is
because in Britain and the Commonwealth, and to a lesser
extent in North America, a third meaning of the term
Evangelical has emerged since the eighteenth century.

Third, therefore, as Mark Noll, David Bebbington and
George Rawlyk write in their book *Evangelicalism*, Evangelical

is 'the best word available to describe a fairly discrete network of Protestant Christian Movements arising from the eighteenth century in Great Britain and its colonies'.[1] They further argue that what identifies these movements as distinctive is 'a consistent pattern of convictions and attitudes' and in a fourfold definition that has won wide acceptance they define these as:

> biblicism (a reliance on the Bible as ultimate religious authority), conversionism (a stress on the new birth), activism (an energetic, individualistic approach to religious duties and social involvement), and crucicentrism (a focus on Christ's redeeming work as the heart of essential Christianity).[2]

In his essay 'Evangelical Theology should be Evangelical', John Stackhouse argues that the Evangelical emphasis on these four convictions has meant that Evangelicalism has also been marked by a fifth distinctive quality, what he describes as 'transdenominationalism':

> evangelicals place special emphasis on this constellation of four and do so in such a way as to relativize every other conviction. There is nothing in the generic evangelical impulse that militates directly against denominational distinctives and divisions, but there is an important ecumenical dynamic to the elevating of these four convictions as nonnegotiable elements of Christian profession and practice, and therefore are willing to negotiate, or even simply to leave to each Christian community, decisions regarding all other issues of dispute, which are seen as secondary and nonessential. This transdenominationalism, therefore, is the fifth evangelical quality to round out our list.[3]

I think the point made by Stackhouse in this quotation is a valid one, and so what we shall be considering in this chapter is the heritage of those whose understanding and practice of Christianity can be traced back to the religious revival of the mid-eighteenth century, and conforms to the fivefold definition of biblicism, conversionism, activism, crucicentrism and transdenominationalism I have just outlined.

2. The heritage of Evangelicalism

In all too many discussions of Evangelicalism there is an implicit assumption that the heritage Evangelicalism has received from the past is a set of theological beliefs that are to be defended at all costs and against all comers. As a result the question of whether any given individual is or is not an Evangelical tends all too often to be reduced to the question of whether they are willing to subscribe to a particular set of doctrines, such as, for example, those contained in the Universities and Colleges Christian Fellowship (UCCF) statement of faith.[4]

It would, I think, be impossible to deny that widely shared theological beliefs are a central part of the heritage that Evangelicalism has received from its past. As we have already noted, a particular set of theological convictions that Evangelicals have inherited from their forebears are what make Evangelicals a distinctive part of the wider Christian community. However, I think it would also be a mistake to define the heritage of Evangelicalism solely in terms of the theological tenets that Evangelicals have in common. This is for two reasons.

First, the theological heritage of Evangelicalism does not just embrace those beliefs that Evangelicals have in common but also those beliefs on which they differ. The theological heritage of Evangelicalism is not simple and agreed: it is complex, pluriform and disputed.

Second, the heritage of Evangelicalism consists of a good deal more than simply a set of theological beliefs. It also consists of the histories of groups and individuals, and various traditions of spirituality, worship, hymnody and missionary activity, as well as a set of social and political attitudes. The words 'histories' and 'traditions' are important here because they reflect the fact that, just as the theological heritage of Evangelicalism is pluriform, so is its heritage in all these other areas as well. In the remainder of this section of this paper I shall go on to look at each of these points in more detail.

The theological heritage of Evangelicalism

The points I have just made about the theological heritage of Evangelicalism can be illustrated by reference to the Evangelical Alliance Basis of Faith. This runs as follows:

> Evangelical Christians accept the revelation of the triune God given in the Scriptures of the Old and New Testaments and confess the historic faith of the Gospel therein set forth.
>
> They here assert doctrines that they regard as crucial to the understanding of the faith, and which should issue in mutual love, practical Christian service and evangelistic concern.
>
> ● The sovereignty and grace of God, the Father, God the Son and God the Holy Spirit in creation, providence, revelation, redemption and final judgement.
>
> ● The divine inspiration of the Holy Scripture and its consequent entire trustworthiness and supreme authority in all matters of faith and conduct.
>
> ● The universal sinfulness and guilt of fallen man, making him subject to God's wrath and condemnation.
>
> ● The substitutionary sacrifice of the incarnate Son of God as the sole all sufficient ground of redemption from the guilt and power of sin and from its eternal consequences.
>
> ● The justification of the sinner solely by the grace of God through faith in Christ crucified and risen from the dead.
>
> ● The illuminating, regenerating, indwelling and sanctifying work of God the Holy Spirit.
>
> ● The priesthood of all believers, who form the universal Church, the Body of which Christ is the Head and which is

committed by His command to the proclamation of the
Gospel throughout the world.

● The expectation of the personal, visible return of the Lord
Jesus Christ in power and glory.[5]

This statement of faith reflects the fact that Evangelicals do
have a central core of beliefs that they hold in common and
that they regard as theologically non-negotiable. On the other
hand, it also reveals the complex and pluriform nature of
Evangelical theology, both in what it says and in what it does
not say.

In terms of what it does say the point to note is that the
present statement of faith is only the latest in a series of statements of faith produced by the Evangelical Alliance during the
course of its history.[6] Each of these is slightly different and
each very carefully worded so as to achieve maximum agreement in the face of Evangelical theological disunity. That is to
say, the various recensions of the Evangelical Alliance's statement of faith not only reflect the fact that there are things that
Evangelicals have held in common theologically, but also
reflect the fact that they have disagreed theologically and *precisely for this reason* have had to develop a form of words that
would allow them to confess the faith together in the face of
this disagreement.

In terms of what the statement does not say the point to
note is that for each of the points of agreement mentioned
there are lots of points of historic theological disagreement
between Evangelicals that are not mentioned. Three examples
will serve to substantiate this point.

First, on the subject of Holy Scripture, while Evangelicals
have agreed about the inspiration and authority of Scripture,
it is also clear that they have disagreed on the questions of
whether the inspiration of Scripture implies that Scripture is
free from all forms of error, how Scripture should be interpreted and whether Scripture provides a complete blueprint
for matters concerning church government and the Christian
life.

Second, on the subject of the Holy Spirit, while Evangelicals have agreed about the fact that the Holy Spirit illuminates, regenerates, indwells and sanctifies the believer, they have disagreed about the degree of sanctification that the believer can expect to enjoy this side of heaven, and about whether the miraculous gifts of the Holy Spirit referred to in the New Testament[7] are still available to the church today.

Third, on the subject of eschatology, while Evangelicals have agreed about the personal and visible return of Christ, they have disagreed about other matters such as whether there will be a millennial reign of Christ on earth[8] and whether this will precede or follow the second coming, and the nature of the eternal damnation that will be experienced by the unfaithful after the last judgement.

These examples could be multiplied almost indefinitely and they all illustrate the fact that it would be misleading to depict the theological heritage of Evangelicalism simply in terms of those beliefs concerning which there has been general agreement among Evangelicals. The fact is that Evangelicalism, like other Christian theological traditions such as Roman Catholicism, Lutheranism and Eastern Orthodoxy, has always been pluriform and as a result the nature of Evangelical theology has always been a contested issue.[9]

The wider heritage of Evangelicalism

As I have already indicated, there is a good deal more to the heritage of Evangelicalism than simply a theological tradition.

Evangelical histories First, Evangelicals are heirs to a long and complex history, which continues to shape the nature of Evangelicalism today. For example, Evangelicalism in the Church of England has been shaped by the original Evangelical revival in the eighteenth century, conflict with Roman and Anglo-Catholicism, conflict with theological liberalism, the rise and decline of 'liberal Evangelicalism', the impact of the charismatic movement, and evangelistic and missionary activity at home and overseas.

Furthermore, because history is shaped by the activity and influence of individuals, Evangelicalism in the Church of England has also been shaped by the lives of individual Evangelical leaders ranging from William Grimshaw in the eighteenth century through John Charles Ryle in the nineteenth century to John Stott in the twentieth, as well as by the lives of Evangelicals from other denominations such as C.H. Spurgeon or D.M. Lloyd-Jones.

What is true of the Evangelicalism in the Church of England is also true of Evangelicalism within other denominations and in other parts of the world. Each of these forms of Evangelicalism has its own distinctive history, and each of them has been shaped by the influence and activity of their own Evangelical leaders as well as by Evangelicals from other churches. Moreover, the historical pattern is complicated still further by the transdenominational character of Evangelicalism, reflected in the existence of bodies such as the Evangelical Alliance, UCCF and Scripture Union, which have crossed denominational boundaries, and which have had their own histories and their own leaders.

What this has meant is that, just as the theological heritage of Evangelicalism has been pluriform, so also has its history. The various historical influences that have shaped Evangelicalism and the different beliefs and practices of influential individuals within it have meant that Evangelicalism has never been a static and homogeneous phenomenon but has been a constantly changing tradition that has developed in a whole variety of different (and sometimes contradictory) ways.

Evangelical spiritualities Second, part of the pluriformity that has marked Evangelical history has been the pluriform nature of Evangelical spirituality.

'Spirituality' is a rather imprecise word that is used in a variety of different ways, but I am using it here to refer to what Bradley Holt, in his *Brief History of Christian Spirituality*, calls the 'particular style of discipleship' followed by Evangelical Christians.[10] In other words, I am talking about the ways in which Evangelicals have sought to respond to the gospel in the way that they have lived their lives.

What soon becomes obvious to any student of Evangelical history is that one has to talk about the 'ways' in which Evangelicals have responded, because their patterns of discipleship have been many and various. If, for instance, one compares the patterns of discipleship practised by an eighteenth-century Methodist, a nineteenth-century Evangelical Quaker and a late twentieth-century member of a Southern Californian 'mega church', significant differences will soon become apparent.

Two clear examples of the diversity of Evangelical spirituality that illustrate the sorts of differences to which I have been referring are provided by differing Evangelical approaches to the issues of 'worldliness' and the contemporary work of the Holy Spirit.

Over the centuries many Evangelical Christians have held that a very clear distinction can be made between Christian and 'worldly' behaviour and that consistent Christian discipleship means strict avoidance of the latter. For example, Oliver Barclay notes that within British Evangelicalism in the years before the Second World War:

> There was also a strong tendency to legalism about conduct. Drink, tobacco, the cinema and theatre, make-up and dancing were all generally taboo. DJ used to relate how, as a schoolboy with an uncertain conscience, he dared to go to a theatre. When he was met by a notice saying 'To the Pit', he decided that he must make his rapid escape! No responsible evangelical would be seen going into a pub, though pubs were admittedly very different from what they are today. Relationships between the sexes were extremely restrained. In fact it was difficult for young people to get to know one another, as 'going out' was frowned on unless it was already 'serious'.[11]

This kind of legalistic spirituality had a long pedigree in British and North American Evangelicalism, and was also a feature of churches in other parts of the world that had been founded by Evangelical missionary activity. However, it was never universally accepted (the great C.H. Spurgeon, for example, had a strong liking for tobacco!), and in the last fifty years it has been widely abandoned by British and North American Evangelicals.

This does not mean that the distinction between Christian and 'worldly' behaviour has been abandoned, but that the line between the two is generally now seen as much less clear cut than was once the case. An alternative form of Evangelical spirituality has developed that would say that it is permissible to engage in activities that were previously seen as taboo providing that this is done in a responsible and godly fashion. Thus drinking alcohol would be acceptable providing that it does not result in drunkenness; relationships with the other sex would be encouraged providing that they did not lead to extramarital sexual activity; and going to the cinema would be a perfectly good thing to do providing that what was seen was not pornographic, violent or blasphemous.

It is also the case that for much of Evangelical history the work of the Holy Spirit in the life of a Christian was seen in terms of His enabling us to know God and to share the new life Christ won for us through His death and resurrection. For example, in his 1886 lectures on Christian doctrine, the American Evangelical theologian Archibald Hodge declared that:

> the immanent Holy Ghost makes God the Father and God the Son, and so Christ the God-man, now glorified in heaven, omnipresent to all the Church in heaven and on earth. If the Holy Ghost were withdrawn, the Christ would be absent and of none effect in us. But if the Holy Ghost is present and effective in us, we dwell in the full flood of the light and the life of God and of his Christ.[12]

What there is no reference to in Hodge's work is the idea that the same kind of miraculous activity of the Holy Spirit that can be found in the New Testament should also be expected to be a part of Christian life today. Hodge's work reflects the almost universal Evangelical consensus that this miraculous activity was needed to accredit the Christ and the Apostles, but being no longer needed it then ceased (the so-called 'cessationist' position).[13]

This cessationist position came to be increasingly challenged as the result of the growth of the worldwide Pentecostal movement in the wake of the Azusa street revival of 1906. Pentecostal theology was initially rejected by most Evangelicals, but a belief in continuing miraculous manifestations of the Holy Spirit became a widespread part of mainstream Evangelicalism as a result of the growth of the charismatic movement from the 1960s onwards.[14]

However, as I have indicated above, Evangelicals have continued to disagree theologically about this matter, with the result that there are now two distinct strands of Evangelical spirituality. One of these sees the work of the Holy Spirit in traditional terms, resulting in the conversion of sinners and their subsequent growth in faith and holiness. The other strand would agree with this but would want to add that we should be looking for the miraculous activity of the Spirit to be manifested in phenomena such as speaking in tongues, prophecy, words of knowledge, deliverance ministry and the ministry of healing.

Evangelical worship Third, a further part of the pluriformity of Evangelicalism has been a pluriformity of forms of worship. One of the traits that most clearly reflects both the transdenominational character of Evangelicalism and the difference between charismatic and non-charismatic spirituality is the wide diversity of ways of worshipping God, both historically and today.

Down the centuries there has been no one standard Evangelical form of worship. Because of its Protestant heritage, Evangelical worship has normally been in the vernacular. It has also avoided practices associated with Roman Catholic theology, such as the veneration of statues, relics and icons, the use of candles or incense, anything that would suggest the sacrifice of the Mass, and the offering of prayers to the saints or for the departed. But these features apart, diversity has been the norm.

- Evangelical worship has been both liturgical and non-liturgical.

- It has often involved hymnody, but there have been some Evangelical traditions (such as the Evangelical Quaker tradition) where hymns have not generally been used.

- It has often been very heavily dominated by the role of the ordained minister, but there have been forms of Evangelicalism where there are no ordained ministers and the congregation as whole is responsible under God for how the service proceeds (as in the case of Brethren services).

- Some traditions have emphasized the importance of lengthy expository sermons, but in other traditions a more narrative or 'story'-based style of preaching is the norm. In still others the tradition would be for a variety of members of the congregation to bring a testimony or a word from the Lord.

- In some traditions the Lord's Supper has been celebrated once a quarter whereas in others it has been celebrated every week.

- In some Evangelical churches women have been expected to keep silent whereas in others they have been permitted to take a full part in services and even lead them.

Evangelical hymnody Fourth, diversity has also been the norm for Evangelical hymnody. While Evangelicals have generally obeyed St Paul's injunction to address 'one another in psalms and hymns and spiritual songs, singing and making melody to the Lord with all your heart' (Ephesians 5:19), the musical forms in which they have done so have varied widely.

If, for a moment, we focus on British Evangelicalism, we find that its musical heritage includes unaccompanied Psalmody, the classic Evangelical hymns of Charles Wesley, John Newton and William Cowper, the 'Sacred Songs and Solos' of Ira Sankey, the reworked music hall songs of the

Salvation Army and the more recent music associated with the charismatic revival such as the music produced by Graham Kendrick. If we then widen the picture to include Evangelicalism worldwide, the picture becomes even more complex and diverse, embracing everything from Christian country and western music in the United States to music in a variety of local idioms and traditions in the two-thirds world. The types of instruments used have been equally varied, ranging from organs and harmoniums through brass bands and rock bands to the native musical instruments used by Evangelical Christians in the two-thirds world.

Evangelical Missionary Activity Fifth, as part of that activism that is one of their defining characteristics, Evangelicals have always been keen to share their faith with both their immediate neighbours and with those in other parts of the world. However, the ways in which they have attempted to do this have been many and varied.

As well as direct one-to-one witnessing to unconverted relatives, friends and neighbours, they have also practised itinerant evangelism, parish-based evangelism, crusade evangelism, and the kind of more low-key, relational type of evangelism associated with the currently popular Alpha programme. In terms of overseas missionary work Evangelicals have worked with denominational missionary societies such as the Church Missionary Society or the Baptist Missionary Society and independent transdenominational missionary agencies such as the Overseas Missionary Fellowship, and have even, on occasion, simply set off on their own, as in the famous cases of Hudson Taylor and Gladys Aylward.

Both at home and overseas, Evangelicals have also employed a variety of methods to get the gospel message across. These have included not only direct personal testimony and traditional evangelistic sermons, but also book and tract distribution, magic lantern shows, films, radio and television broadcasts, videos and, most recently, the use of Internet web sites. You name it, and some enterprising Evangelical has probably tried it!

As well as witnessing to the population at large, Evangelical evangelistic activity has also been targeted at specific groups such as prisoners, members of the armed forces, railway workers, students, schoolchildren and other groups too numerous to mention, with the production of materials and the holding of events suitable for the particular group in question.

In addition to the diversity of evangelistic approaches just described, there has been a further diversity among Evangelicals on a variety of other issues to do with missionary activity.

- They have differed on whether it is right to invite people to respond to the gospel at the end of evangelistic events or whether this puts people under undue pressure and leads to premature confessions of faith that do not bear lasting fruit.

- They have differed on whether it is right to engage in joint missionary activity with non-Evangelicals or whether this leads to theological compromise and confusion. For example, D.M. Lloyd-Jones and a number of others who thought like him refused to endorse the Billy Graham missions in Great Britain because Graham was willing to share a platform with non-Evangelicals.[15]

- They have differed on the link between evangelism and social action. Some Evangelicals have felt that a clear distinction needs to be made between the two, both because nothing is said about the latter in the great commission in Matthew 28:18–20, and because of a fear that the gospel message will come to be identified with a message of social improvement. Other Evangelicals, however, have argued that evangelism and social action need to go together both because social action helps to make the gospel credible and because of the biblical mandate to care for the poor and the oppressed.

- The Lausanne Covenant produced by the International Congress on World Evangelization in 1974 affirmed that evangelism and social action needed to go together,[16] and there is now a widespread Evangelical consensus on this point, but the two different approaches I have just outlined remain part of the Evangelical heritage.

● Finally, as part of the wider debate about the work of the Holy Spirit referred to above, Evangelicals have differed on whether the Bible indicates that, in order to be fully effective, evangelism needs to be accompanied by miraculous 'signs and wonders'. This position was taken by John Wimber and the Vineyard churches and was advocated by Wimber in his influential books *Power Evangelism* and *Power Healing*.[17] Other Evangelicals, however, remain unconvinced. Thus John Stott writes in his recent book Evangelical Truth: 'we should certainly be open to miracles (because God is the Creator), but we have no right to expect miracles with the same frequency with which they occurred in special biblical periods (because ours is not an epoch of revelation)'.[18]

Evangelical Social and Political Attitudes Sixth, another aspect of their activism has been the conviction of many Evangelicals that it is important to get involved in tackling the ills facing society as a whole. The classic examples are the campaign for the abolition of the slave trade led by William Wilberforce at the beginning of the nineteenth century and the numerous campaigns for social improvement in Britain led by the Earl of Shaftesbury later on in the same century.

However, it would be misleading to see the approaches of Wilberforce and Shaftesbury as typical of Evangelicalism as a whole. This is because alongside those who have campaigned for social and political change and transformation there have also been those who have been socially and politically conservative, who supported the social and political status quo, and have felt that concern for the poor and the oppressed was best expressed through individual acts of charity. Furthermore, it also needs to be noted that Evangelicals have taken different sides on specific political issues. The diversity of the

Evangelical heritage on these points can be seen if we look at three examples of Evangelical social and political attitudes in specific situations.

The first example is Evangelical attitudes to political and social change in the United States of America. In his important study *Discovering an Evangelical Heritage* Donald Dayton notes that in the years leading up to the American Civil War many American Evangelicals were influenced by the teaching of the Evangelical preacher and theologian Charles Finney, who held that the church's calling to attack sin meant working for the transformation of society:

> Now the great business of the church is to reform the world – to put away every kind of sin. The church of Christ was originally organized to be a body of reformers. The very profession of Christianity implies the profession and virtually an oath to do all that can be done for the universal reformation of the world. The Christian church was designed to make aggressive movements in every direction – to lift up her voice and put forth her energies against iniquity in high and low places – to reform individuals, communities and governments, and never rest until the kingdom and the greatness of the kingdom under the whole heaven shall be given to the people of the saints of the most high God – until every form of iniquity shall be driven from the earth.[19]

In the American context, this vision for the reformation of society led many Evangelicals to take practical action to help the poor and the oppressed, and, in particular, to become involved in the struggle for the abolition of slavery both through political campaigning and through direct action, such as the economic boycott of slave-produced goods and giving assistance to fugitive slaves, even when this was against the law. Furthermore, as Dayton points out, the same egalitarian interpretation of Scripture that led these Evangelicals to support the abolition of slavery also led them to campaign for the equality of women with men both in the church and in society as a whole.[20]

After the Civil War, however, this politically active and socially liberal form of Evangelicalism became eclipsed by an alternative form, which stressed the conversion of individual souls rather than the reformation of society, and which was socially and politically conservative. It is this latter strand of Evangelicalism that has remained dominant in the United States to this day, which explains why so much of American Evangelicalism is associated with right-wing politics, and why Evangelicals largely opposed both the civil rights movement in the 1960s and the growth of contemporary feminism. According to Dayton, this change had two roots.[21] First, Finney's vision of a transformed Protestant America became difficult to sustain as America became more secular and more religiously plural. Second, his vision was rooted theologically in both a postmillennial eschatology that held that the world as a whole would be transformed into God's kingdom prior to the return of Christ, and in a strong Wesleyan emphasis on the power of the Spirit to overcome sin at both a personal and social level. The form of Evangelicalism that became dominant after the Civil War, however, was shaped by a combination of a premillennial eschatology that held that the world would grow more evil prior to Christ's return and a Calvinist emphasis on the continuing power of sin in both the believer and the world, emanating from Princeton Theological Seminary.

The second example of divergent social and political attitudes comes from South Africa. On the one hand, Evangelical missionaries in the Cape Colony at the beginning of the nineteenth century preached the equality of black and white people before God and were instrumental in the abolition of slavery in the colony. More recently, during the apartheid era, South African Evangelicals such as Michael Cassidy worked hard to try to achieve reconciliation between the races and social and political change, and they were supported in their efforts by visiting Evangelicals such as John Stott and Michael Green. Thus Michael Green used an invitation to speak to a series of evening meetings at the University of Stellenbosch to criticize the failure of the church to oppose apartheid and was then barred from speaking again for the rest of the week on the grounds that he had 'abused the pulpit by speaking of politics'.[22]

On the other hand, it also has to be acknowledged that many Evangelicals – in the Dutch Reformed Church and in other churches as well – either supported the apartheid regime, or at least failed to oppose it. This was either because they accepted the theology of racial separation upon which the ideology of apartheid was based; or because they accepted the argument of the South African government that apartheid was necessary to protect Christian civilization against the threat of communist subversion; or because they believed that the church should not get involved in politics, but should concentrate on issues of personal morality and direct charitable help to those in need.

The third example of divergent social and political attitudes is provided by Evangelical attitudes to the problems in the Middle East. On the one hand, many British and Arab Evangelicals are supportive of the Palestinian cause and are critical either of the Israeli occupation of the West Bank and the Gaza Strip or of the very existence of the state of Israel as a specifically Jewish state.[23] The Syrian Evangelical Chawkat Moucarry writes, for example, that 'The establishment of Israel on Arab land was an immense injustice' and declares that the Zionist dream of a Jewish homeland should be abandoned in favour of 'one secular and democratic state for all'.[24]

On the other hand, since the beginning of the nineteenth century, many Evangelicals in both Britain and North America have held that there should be a restored Jewish state on the land promised by God to Abraham and have therefore been strongly supportive both of the growth of the Zionist movement and of the present state of Israel since its foundation in 1948. Their influence is one of the factors that helps to explain the strong support for Israel by subsequent administrations in the United States. For many of these Evangelicals the basis of their support for Zionism has been a dispensationalist theology which holds that God has a continuing covenant with the Jewish people that is separate from His covenant with the Christian church. Some have held to an eschatology in which the establishment of a third Jewish temple and a consequent devastating Middle East war are a necessary prelude to the return of Christ.[25]

What these three examples clearly demonstrate is that the social and political heritage of Evangelicalism is one that is deeply divided. There has not been a unified Evangelical approach to social and political issues any more than there has been a unified approach to any of the other issues we have considered.

3. Evaluating the Evangelical Heritage(s)

The need to be honest

If we are to learn to evaluate the Evangelical heritage in a responsible fashion the first thing we need to do is to acknowledge the diversity that I have sketched out above. That is to say, we have to acknowledge that there is not one single unified Evangelical heritage, but a series of different heritages that both overlap and diverge from each other in a very complex fashion.

The impression is sometimes given that the diversity of contemporary Evangelicalism is a modern phenomenon that is the result of a decline from some previous golden age when all Evangelicals were in agreement about what Evangelicalism stood for. This impression is completely misleading. There never has been a period throughout Evangelical history from the eighteenth century onwards in which there has not been disagreement and disunity among Evangelicals. Two consequences follow from this.

First, we need to be prepared to admit that none of us is simply an Evangelical without further qualification. Although it is possible and helpful to identify the common characteristics of Evangelicals in the way outlined at the beginning of this paper, it is also necessary to note that those who share these characteristics embody them in a variety of different ways, which reflect both their divergent heritages and their own particular theological and spiritual pilgrimages.

What this means is that all of us who are Evangelicals are 'hyphenated Evanglicals'. We are all Anglican-Evangelicals, or

Baptist-Evangelicals, or Calvinist-Evangelicals, or Charismatic-Evangelicals, or whatever, and we need to be open about this fact and not either covertly or overtly try to hijack the label Evangelical so that it refers to our kind of Evangelicalism alone.

Second, we need to be very cautious about the oft-repeated claim that 'evangelical Christianity is original, apostolic, New Testament Christianity'.[26] If what is meant by this is that the central theological beliefs Evangelicals hold in common, such as the authority of Scripture and justification by grace alone through Christ alone by faith alone, are also beliefs that are central to the teaching of the New Testament, then the claim is defensible. However, if we go beyond this and try to claim that Evangelicalism as a historical phenomenon is identical with the Christianity of the New Testament, then we run into severe difficulties. Either we have to admit that it is not Evangelicalism as such but our own particular version of it that we are talking about, or we have to say that New Testament Christianity, like Evangelicalism, was radically pluriform in nature (a claim that Evangelicals have not generally wanted to accept because of its implication for the notion of Biblical authority).

The need for serious theological engagement with our Evangelical heritages

There are three ways of approaching the heritages of Evangelicalism.

The first way is to simply regard these heritages as interesting for their own sake, but as having nothing to say to us today. For example, in a letter written in January 1775, the English Evangelical John Newton explains that if he should:

> suggest in some companies, that the conversion of a hundred sinners (more or less) to God is an event of more real importance than the temporal prosperity of the greatest nation on earth I should be charged with ignorance and arrogance; but your Lordship is skilled in scriptural arithmetic, which alone can teach us to estimate the value of souls, and will agree with

me, that one soul is worth more than the whole world, on account of its redemption-price, its vast capacities, and its duration. Should we suppose a nation to consist of forty millions, the whole and each individual to enjoy as much good as this life can afford, without abatement, for a term of fifty years each – all this good, or an equal quantity, might be exhausted by a single person in two thousand millions of years, which would be but a moment in comparison of the eternity which would still follow. And if this good were merely temporal good, the whole aggregate of it would be evil and misery, if compared with that happiness in God, of which only they who are made partakers of a divine life are capable.[27]

It would be possible to note what Newton says in this quotation, observe that it presents us with an example of an apolitical and otherworldly piety, and then think nothing more about it. The problem with this approach is that it would fail to take seriously the possibility that what Newton says might in fact be true and that we might need to modify our belief and behaviour as a result.

The second way to approach our Evangelical heritages is to regard these heritages as possessing binding authority. In terms of the quotation from Newton this would entail the belief that because he is a recognized Evangelical theologian what he says must be correct and as such binding upon us. It might be argued that no one would in fact take this approach, but in fact there has been a recurring tendency to give *de facto* authority to Evangelical theologians akin the authority accorded to the doctors of the church in the Roman Catholic tradition. Thus people will quote from Newton, or John Wesley, or Charles Spurgeon, or more recently D.M. Lloyd-Jones, John Stott or J.I. Packer, as if what they have to say settled the matter in question.

The problem with this approach is twofold. First, it runs foul of that Evangelical diversity that this paper has highlighted. Not all recognized Evangelical theologians can be correct because they do not all teach the same things. Second, and more seriously, it means forgetting that only Scripture is infallible, and that, as sinful human beings, even the best

Evangelical thinkers will often get things wrong, and will therefore be misleading if taken as a guide.

This means we have to approach their work critically, asking about the weaknesses as well as the strengths of their teachings. In the case of Newton, for example, we can legitimately ask if he has given enough weight to the spiritual importance of political and social issues and whether his otherworldly emphasis might not encourage people to neglect to try to change society to reflect more closely the values of God's kingdom.

The third and preferable approach is the approach of serious critical engagement. With this approach the need to take seriously and to be challenged by what previous generations of Evangelicals have believed and taught about Christian belief and behaviour is properly acknowledged, but due acknowledgement is also given to the fact that what they have believed and taught may have been wrong.

The shape of serious theological engagement with our Evangelical heritages

The final question that now has to be answered is what such an engagement would look like. Revealing my true colours as an *Anglican*-Evangelical I want to argue that such an engagement has to be based on the right use of Scripture, tradition and reason.

Scripture has to be the primary basis for such an engagement, not simply because an Evangelical theology that was not based on the Bible would be so divergent from the Evangelical tradition as to be a contradiction in terms, but because, as God's inspired word (2 Timothy 3:16), produced by those who spoke from God because they were moved by the Holy Spirit (2 Peter 1:21), the Bible is by its very nature the supreme theological authority because it carries the authority of God Himself.[28]

However, the Bible is a very large and complex collection of different materials produced at different times and in different genres. What, therefore, gives it the coherence that enables it to function as a theological authority for us? I would argue that the answer to this question is that what gives coherence to the biblical witness is its evangelical character.

What I mean by this is that the Bible has coherence because when it is properly understood it can be seen to bear witness in all its diversity to the 'good news' (the *euaggelion* – Mark 1:15; Romans 1:1) about the free grace of God the Father that has been manifested in and through God the Son in the power of God the Holy Spirit. As the great Swiss theologian Karl Barth puts it, the message of the Bible is that:

> In His free grace, God is for man in every respect; He surrounds man from all sides. He is man's Lord who is before him, above him, after him, and thence also with him in history, the locus of man's existence. Despite man's insignificance, God is with him as his Creator who intended and made mankind to be very good. Despite man's sin, God is with him, the One who was in Jesus Christ reconciling the world, drawing man unto Himself in merciful judgment. Man's evil past is not merely crossed out because of its irrelevancy. Rather, it is in the good care of God. Despite man's life in the flesh, corrupt and ephemeral God is with him. The victory in Christ is here and now present through his Spirit, man's strength, companion and comfort. Despite man's death God is with him, meeting him as redeemer and perfecter at the threshold of the future to show him the totality of existence in the true light in which the eyes of God beheld it from the beginning and will behold it evermore. In what He is for man and does for man, God ushers in the history leading to the ultimate salvation of man.[29]

The first question that has to be asked of the heritages of Evangelicalism is therefore the radical question: to what extent do they bear witness to this evangelical message of God's free grace and enable women and men to respond to it in thankful obedience?

In asking this question we also have to engage in a constant dialectic between the whole of the Bible and its individual parts. That is to say, it is the overall message of God's free

grace that must provide the context for understanding the separate parts of the biblical material, but each individual verse
has to be taken seriously in order to enable us to understand
the overall biblical message in all its richness and fullness.

Therefore, as Evangelicals have rightly insisted down the
centuries, we do have to engage in detailed biblical exegesis,
testing Evangelical belief and practice against both the Bible as
a whole and the individual parts of the biblical narrative,
using the best historical and linguistic tools available to us.

As well as engaging with the primary witness of Scripture
we also have to take seriously the secondary witness of those
who down the centuries have also sought to understand and
explain the biblical message and to live it out in their lives.
This is what is meant by the 'tradition' of the church and we
need to take it seriously because nothing could be more arrogant than to suppose that either we ourselves or the particular
strand of Evangelicalism in which we stand has a monopoly in
the right understanding of what the Bible says or how we
should respond to it.

Furthermore, we cannot even assume that Evangelicalism
as such has a monopoly on theological wisdom. We need to
explore not only our Evangelical heritages but also what has
come to be known as the 'Great Tradition', the witness of the
Christian church as a whole down the ages.[30]

However, as I have already argued with reference to the
work of John Newton, we cannot give absolute authority
to tradition. Tradition, whether Evangelical tradition or the
tradition of some other part of the church, can only ever be a
secondary witness that points beyond itself to the witness of
Scripture. To put it another way, tradition is valuable as a tool
that enables us to understand better what the Bible has to say
and to respond to it in a more appropriate fashion. In so far as
it enables us to do this we should make use of it as a good gift
from God. However, tradition can also obscure the meaning of
Scripture and cause us to respond inappropriately to God.
When we believe that it is doing this we must reject it even if
what we are rejecting carries the most 'orthodox' or
'Evangelical' credentials.

Finally, we must pay attention to reason. 'Reason' can be a bogeyman to many Evangelicals because they fear that the use of reason means elevating human wisdom above Scripture and using it to judge and even to reject what the biblical witness has to say. However, while there are good reasons for rejecting the use of reason in this sense, there are two other uses of the term 'reason' that we do have to take seriously.

The first is the human capacity for rational thought. God has given human beings the ability to use rational thought to discern truth. Indeed, this is one of the distinguishing features of being human.[31] What this means for us is that we have to be prepared to engage in rational disciplined thought when exploring and assessing the heritages of Evangelicalism. We cannot take the attractive but intellectually lazy options of letting others do our thinking for us, or being guided by what seems superficially attractive, or following a line of argument that we know will make us popular. An unswerving commitment to the truth so far as we can discern it has to be our guiding principle.

The second is what the Anglican *Virginia Report* calls the 'mind of a particular culture with its characteristic ways of seeing things, asking about them and explaining them'.[32] We have to take reason in this sense seriously for apologetic reasons. Like St Paul before the Areopagus in Athens (Acts 17:16–33) we have to address contemporary culture in ways that will enable it to make sense of the good news contained in the biblical witness. What this means is that we have to explore the riches of the Evangelical heritages and ask what we can use to enable us to communicate successfully with contemporary culture and, conversely, what things in the Evangelical tradition now present stumbling blocks that prevent such communication taking place.

Conclusion

What we have seen in the course of this paper is that there is not one single Evangelical heritage but a variety of Evangelical heritages that are diverse and even contradictory, not only in theological terms, but also in connection with a whole variety of other issues ranging from spirituality to politics.

It has also been argued that the proper way to respond to this diversity is to engage seriously with this heritage, acknowledging its diversity and assessing it in a theologically responsible fashion in the light of Scripture, reason and tradition, in order that we may better understand, obey and witness to that good news of God's free grace extended to sinners in Jesus Christ, which is the foundation of all evangelical theology that is worthy of its name.

* * *

Dr Martin Davie works for the Church of England as the Theological Consultant to the House of Bishops and the Theological Secretary to the Council for Christian Unity. Prior to taking up his present appointment he was on the staff at Oak Hill Theological College.

Notes

1 M. Noll, D. Bebbington and G. Rawlyk, *Evangelicalism* (Oxford: Oxford University Press, 1994), p. 6.

2 Ibid.

3 J.G. Stackhouse, 'Evangelical Theology should be Evangelical' in J.G. Stackhouse (ed.), *Evangelical Futures* (Leicester: IVP, 2000), p. 42. For an account of how this transdenominationalism has found expression in practice in the work of the Evangelical Alliance, see I. Randall and D. Hilborn, *One Body in Christ* (Carlisle: Paternoster, 2001).

4 The UCCF's statement of faith can be found at www.uccf.org.uk.

5 The Evangelical Alliance Basis of Faith can be found at www.eauk.org.

6 See appendices 1–3 in Randall and Hilborn, *One Body in Christ*, and also appendix 6, which records the closely related Basis of Faith produced by the World Evangelical Fellowship in 1951.

7 See Acts *passim* and 1 Corinthians 12:4–11.

8 See Revelation 20:4–6.

9 For details of theological disagreements among Evangelicals see, for example, Randall and Hilborn, *One Body in Christ* and D.W. Bebbington, *Evangelicalism in Modern Britain: A History from the 1730s to the 1980s* (London and New York: Routledge, 1989).

10 B. Holt, *Brief History of Christian Spirituality* (Oxford: Lion, 1997), p. 18.

11 O. Barclay, *Evangelicalism in Britain 1935–1995* (Leicester: IVP, 1997), p. 25. 'DJ' refers to Douglas Johnson, who was the first secretary of the Inter-Varsity Fellowship (the original name for what became UCCF).

12 A.A. Hodge, *Evangelical Theology* (Edinburgh: Banner of Truth, 1976), pp. 112–13.

13 The classic Evangelical statement of this position remains B.B. Warfield, *Counterfeit Miracles* (Edinburgh: Banner of Truth, 1972).

14 See P. Hocken, *Streams of Renewal* (Carlisle: Paternoster, 1997) and H. Cox, *Fire from Heaven* (London: Cassell, 1996).

15 See I.H. Murray, *Evangelicalism Divided* (Edinburgh: Banner of Truth, 2000), ch. 2.

16 See T. Dudley-Smith, *John Stott: A Global Ministry* (Leicester: IVP, 2001), ch. 7.

17 J. Wimber and K. Springer, *Power Evangelism* (London: Hodder & Stoughton, 1985) and *Power Healing* (London: Hodder & Stoughton, 1985).

18 J. Stott, *Evangelical Truth* (Leicester: IVP, 1999), p. 127.

19 C.G. Finney, 'Letters on Revival' no. 23 in D.W. Dayton, *Discovering an Evangelical Heritage* (Peabody, Massachusetts: Hendrickson, 1994), p. 21.

20 Ibid., ch. 8.

21 Ibid., ch. 10.

22 E.M.B. Green, *Adventure of Faith* (Grand Rapids, Michigan: Zondervan, 2001), p. 319.

23 See, for example, C. Chapman, *Whose Promised Land?* (Oxford: Lion, 2002) and C. Moucarry, *Faith to Faith: Christianity and Islam in Dialogue* (Leicester: IVP, 2001).

24 Moucarry, *Faith to Faith*, pp. 278, 281.

25 For detailed documentation on Christian Zionism and its theological basis, see Stephen Sizer's forthcoming Middlesex University PhD thesis, *The Promised Land: A Critical Investigation of Evangelical Christian Zionism in Britain and the United States since 1800.*

26 Stott, *Evangelical Truth*, p. 16.

27 J. Newton, *Collected Letters* (London: Hodder & Stoughton, 1989), p. 113.

28 See J.W. Wenham, *Christ and the Bible* (Leicester: Tyndale Press, 1972) for a clear exposition and defence of the position on biblical authority adopted here.

29 K. Barth, *The Humanity of God* (Glasgow: Fontana, 1967), p. 69.

30 See A.E. McGrath, 'Engaging the Great Tradition' in Stackhouse (ed.), *Evangelical Futures*, ch. 5.

31 See C. S. Lewis, *Miracles* (Glasgow: Collins/Fontana, 1985) for this argument.

32 *The Official Report of the Lambeth Conference 1998* (Harrisburg, Pennsylvania: Morehouse, 1999), p. 32.

2

Evangelicals and Social Justice

Andy Hartropp

Introduction

'Social justice' is often a somewhat slippery term, but it is to do with the poor, the needy and those who are less well off in society. To what extent do the poor, the needy and the less well off share in the good things that the rest of society enjoys? That is a question of social justice. Some people on the political right (libertarians) may argue that social justice (as defined here) is a misguided concern, for example, because the distribution of wealth is best left to 'market forces' (though with a safety net for the poorest). But they would not dispute the basic definition as given here.

The basic 'social justice' question (as above) begs many other questions, such as those involving means (for example, is a welfare state the best way to help the poor?) as well as ends. But those have to be put to one side for now, because first there is a fundamental issue that must be addressed in this chapter. Is social justice a legitimate gospel concern? Or, put another way, should evangelicals be particularly bothered about social justice?

If we *are* to be actively concerned about social justice then this will involve (among other things) politics. How society treats its less well off members necessarily involves the political (that is, governmental) dimension, if only to say that laws need to be in place (and enforced) that protect the poor, needy and weak from exploitation by the strong and powerful. However, some Christians who wear the 'Evangelical' label argue that politics and social justice should not be central concerns for Christians. Consider a letter published in the April 2002 issue of the monthly UK newspaper *Evangelicals Now*. The writer argues, among other things, that the kingdom of God is different from the kingdoms of this world. He says:

> Jesus, in a time full of great political/religious questions of 'state and church', remained decisively and distinctly apolitical ... Also, the letters to the churches, and the rest of the New Testament, are firmly in this suit: we toe the line, we play our part responsibly... but we don't get preoccupied... Worldly politics should remain peripheral to the Christian.

That writer does not specifically address questions of social justice, but there are plenty of 'Evangelicals' who would argue, along the same lines, that issues of social justice should not preoccupy us, but should rather be peripheral. In other words, they are not gospel concerns.

Well, who is right? This issue cannot be fudged. Is social justice a central concern of the gospel, or is it not?

Creation – Fall – Redemption – Eschatology

It seems wise to commence with a theological framework that seeks to reflect the overall and gospel thrust of the Bible. One could start, alternatively, with specific verses and passages of Scripture, but – at least with regard to social justice – these may raise matters of detail and interpretation with which a short chapter cannot deal adequately. Hence we begin with the familiar and helpful framework of Creation – Fall – Redemption – Eschatology (C–F–R–E), which helps to present God's gospel of redemption to our minds and hearts. Within this overall context some particular Scriptures will be examined in due course. No doubt this framework has weaknesses, but a major strength is that it can enable us to hold together these four very rich themes, which are so prominent in the Bible, and which together tell the gospel story. At the centre of all this is God Himself, the Holy Trinity: in creation, redemption and in the final and glorious eschatological renewal that still awaits. It must be remembered that C–F–R–E is *not* to be understood as presenting four distinct and separate phases in human history. Instead, Creation, Fall, Redemption and Eschatology (God's new and eternal order at the end of this age) are to be seen as four acts in an unfolding – and utterly real – drama. Each act must be seen in the context of all the other three acts. This guiding principle is the same as the principle that must always guide us when studying the Scriptures: read one part of the Bible in the context of the rest of the Bible. This is surely the best way for our thinking, theology and life to be constantly reformed in the light of God's word.

With the aid of the C–F–R–E framework let us again ask the question: is social justice a central concern of the gospel? The four acts of the drama will be briefly considered in turn (although slightly less briefly in the case of Redemption).

Creation

Social justice essentially concerns the extent to which those who are less well off share in the good things enjoyed by everyone else in a community. This, at least, is the broad definition adopted in this chapter – a definition that will be defended on biblical grounds a little later. The biblical emphasis on Creation brings out two additional points.

First, it is plain that the good things available for humanity to enjoy come from God. This immediately requires a theological amendment to the definition of social justice offered earlier. The question is not only the extent to which the poor share in 'good things': it is, more particularly, the extent to which they share in *God's blessings*.

Second, it is clear that the earth, and all that is in it, is God's: it belongs to Him. God is the Creator, the owner and the director of the world and the entire cosmos, as is made plain (for example) by Psalm 24. This truth will jar with followers of today's ruling worldview – secular humanism – but the point is obviously no less valid for that.

Genesis 1 states several times that the world God made was 'good'. Was this a world in which there was social justice? One way to answer the question is to consider the converse possibility: is it conceivable, within a biblical understanding, that any human being would *not* share fully in the utter goodness of God's good (pre-Fall) world? Absolutely not. It is not remotely credible that any man or woman, made in God's image and mandated to rule over God's world, would be left out as poor or needy.

Fall

The Fall does not detract from the truth that God owns and runs His world. Psalm 24 is written in the post-Fall context. But one direct consequence of humanity's rebellion against God is for human relationships, as is plain from Genesis 3 onwards. And one aspect of sin in human relationships is socio-economic injustice and oppression: maltreatment of the poor and needy. The substantial emphasis on this in the Old Testament is very hard to avoid, but a brief reading of, say, the first chapter of Isaiah will bring the point home. (Injustice is a major theme for Isaiah and for many of the prophets: see, for example, Isaiah 58 and 59.)

Redemption

Even before the gospel is brought to our eyes, the biblical material on Creation and Fall makes it plain that social justice is very much in the heart of God. Similarly, the *lack* of social justice is abhorrent to Him. It might seem adequate to draw the matter to a close here, and get on immediately with the task of furthering social justice. But this would clearly fall short of being an *evangelical* approach. What does the gospel of redemption add to what we have already considered?

God's redeeming work begins in the Old Testament, and God's redemption of His people, Israel, is to deliver them from Egypt. From what were they suffering in Egypt? They were enduring socio-economic oppression: they were a weak people in relation to the Egyptians, and the latter treated the Israelites harshly and oppressively. In other words, the people of Israel were enduring social injustice. This is not a mere metaphor for sin. Rather, it was the harsh reality, the very context in which they cried out to the Lord (for example, Exodus 1:11–14, 2:23–25). And the Lord heard them (for example, Exodus 3:7–10).

The people who were suffering were not, of course, *any* people. They were the descendants of Abraham, Isaac and Jacob, to whom God had made and renewed His covenant promises. Thus God's covenantal concern and His concern about Israel's socio-economic oppression come together. This is plain from Exodus 2:24 ff., where God's response to Israel's cry for help is reported: 'God heard their groaning and he remembered his covenant with Abraham, with Isaac and with Jacob. So God looked on the Israelites and was concerned about them.'

That is the context for the Passover meal and deliverance, and for the Lord's mighty redemption of the Israelites out of Egypt. Having delivered them across the Red Sea, the Lord brought them to Himself at Mount Sinai, and called for their covenantal obedience in response to His covenantal mercy and grace (Exodus 19:3–6). In particular, they were to obey the Lord's commandments given through Moses – commandments that were to govern their relationship both with God and with one another.

Not only were the Israelites saved *from* (among other things) social injustice. They were also saved *for* a life of goodness, righteousness and justice – including social justice. A significant number of the Lord's commandments in Exodus, Leviticus and Deuteronomy refer to relationships and behaviour with regard to the poor, the needy and the less well off. God's holy people were to treat each other as He had treated them.

When we turn to the New Testament and to the account of God's redemption through the Lord Jesus Christ there are of course both similarities to and differences from the Old Testament pattern. What God redeems people from is their sin in general and from its consequences in particular. This is the big picture. Taking the Bible as a whole, it would be quite wrong to suggest that social injustice is the primary form that is taken by sin and the consequences of sin. So there is a marked difference between the particular experience of the Israelites in Egypt and the general experience of God's redeemed people across the world.

Nevertheless, social injustice is still a significant aspect and consequence of human sinfulness. It is part of what we are saved from. Jesus evidently had a concern for the poor, the outcast and the weak. There is no need (or space) here to enter into debates about whether 'the poor' (for example, in Luke 6) are the 'economically' poor or the 'spiritually' poor. It is plain from Jesus' own behaviour that His deep compassion for each and for all included a deep concern for those on the margins and fringes of the community. And His warnings to those who were rich – plainly meaning materially rich – and who neglected those in need cannot be missed (for example, Luke 6:24–25, 16:19–31).

Thus the redemption won for us by Jesus – won ultimately by His death and resurrection – includes redemption from social injustice. It is no surprise, then, that social justice is something that is expected to characterize the New Testament people of God. The 'ethics' sections of the epistles and the behaviour of the early church reported in Acts make it crystal clear that right use of riches and the right treatment of the poor, the needy and the less well off were central aspects of being the redeemed people of God in Christ.

Eschatology

In the eschaton, the glorious consummation of the kingdom of God, there will not be even a hint of injustice. Social injustice is a central feature of the city of man, but it will be totally absent in the City of God. Instead it will be a place and a people of perfect justice and goodness, to the glory and praise of God. As 2 Peter 3:13 expresses it, 'in keeping with his [God's] promise we are looking forward to a new heaven and a new earth, the home of righteousness'.

Not only will the coming of Christ bring in the new heaven and earth, the perfect City, the new Jerusalem; it will also bring about God's full and final judgement against all that is evil and unrighteous, including all social injustice. When Christ comes as Judge, to destroy every rule and authority and power (1 Corinthians 15:24), this will include judgement upon economic wrongdoing and oppression. That is plain from the Old Testament prophets (see, for example, Amos 5:10–18; Ezekiel 28:15–23).

Social Justice as a Central Gospel Concern

In the light of the above biblical and theological material, it is clear that evangelicals should regard social justice not as a peripheral issue, but as a central gospel concern. It is vital, however, that the meaning and implications of this conclusion should be clarified. This will be done here by putting forward, and briefly explaining, six propositions.

1. Social justice and social injustice should concern evangelicals deeply

The meaning of this proposition is simply that matters of social justice and social injustice should be heartfelt concerns for those who call themselves evangelical Christians. These are matters that are evidently on the heart of God, and so they should be for us. The injustices of this world are of deep concern to God, and so they should be for us. What the practical implications of this might be are considered below. The point here is simply that these issues should be of deep concern for evangelicals.

The above proposition excludes and prohibits the notion that social justice and injustice involve only this fleeting world and should therefore only be peripheral and not heartfelt concerns. The Bible knows no such disjunction between issues in this world and issues in the next. It is a false and unbiblical dichotomy to say that heaven is our concern and therefore this earth is not. The whole biblical story and worldview, as summarized by the C–F–R–E framework, for example, excludes such a dichotomy.

2. Evangelicals must think, and think biblically, about social justice

A biblical heart and a biblical mind can hardly be separated. Each needs the other. Each is to feed the other. So this second proposition is vitally linked with the first. In order to *have* a heartfelt concern about social justice and injustice, it is necessary to feed our hearts, through our minds, with what God's word tells us about these matters. (This is, of course, what this chapter has been trying to do.)

But there is another element here also. If our thinking is unbiblical, then both our heart and our behaviour will be displeasing to God. Specifically, if our ideas and emphases about social justice are unbiblical, then this will affect adversely the way we feel and the way we act about social justice. Thus we must subject our thinking about these matters to the scrutiny and searchlight of Scripture. It should hardly surprise us if many non-Christian people have wrong ideas and emphases about social justice. Therefore we would be foolish to accept as true everything that any particular non-Christian school of thought says about social justice and injustice. Whatever newspaper we may read, we must subject every author's views on these issues to the Bible. Therefore we ourselves must learn to think biblically.

This, however, is no small or easy task. For decades, Evangelicals in the UK have, by and large, given little attention to the Bible's teaching on social justice and injustice. Our thinking about these matters, therefore, is likely at present to be dominated by secular and unbiblical ideas. There is much renewing of our minds to be done. Clearly this means, primarily, reading and being changed by God's word. But to help us in this we need to start feeding our minds, and thus our hearts, with the writings of people who reflect a more biblical approach to social justice. Who are these people? As with writings on any other topic, we can find that out only by striving, in God's strength, to bring every thought – both our own, and those of others – captive to Christ.

3. Evangelicals must take a prophetic stance against social injustice

The meaning of this proposition is again simple. Where there is blatant wrongdoing in this world, Christians above all people should be those who are sufficiently clear sighted and courageous to speak out against it. This applies to social injustice in the same way that it applies to other forms of blatant wrongdoing. Note the phrase 'blatant wrongdoing': it is not our job, of course, to go around pointing out every speck of sin. But it is our job, as it was of the Old Testament prophets, to speak out against major areas of wrongdoing. It takes only a short amount of reading about or observing the plight of the many desperately poor people in today's world to become convinced that there is much social injustice in our time.

This proposition does *not*, however, require all evangelical Christians – or the church more generally – to provide detailed 'solutions' to the problems of social injustice. For one thing, such 'solutions' may or may not exist. More importantly, however, we cannot all be experts in every field. What *is* desirable, however, is that *some* evangelicals should, according to God's call upon them, develop expert understanding about social justice and injustice.

4. Our gospel proclamation should include the call to live justly

This proposition is an essential complement to the third proposition. If we are only 'against sin' then we distort the gospel. God's call throughout the Bible is for people to turn from sin and to turn to Him in faith and obedience. It is not enough, therefore, to speak out against blatant wrongdoing (whether it be social injustice or something else). The Bible calls us, as repentant and forgiven sinners, to call others also to 'Repent and believe the good news' (Mark 1:15).

In other words, social injustice is part of the sin and wrong-doing that we invite people to be saved *from*, through faith in Christ. And social justice is part of the goodness and right-eousness that we call people to be saved *for*, through faith in Christ. In our evangelism, we do have opportunities to link the gospel in this kind of way to particular areas of wrong-doing, and particular areas of renewal. To a serial bank robber, the gospel call surely includes 'turn from bank robbing'. In the same way, the gospel call to a self-seeking and wealthy Westerner might well include the call to 'turn from your part in social injustice'.

5. Our own churches should model social justice

The words of James 2:1–17 are needed here. Social justice, as we saw earlier, means treating well those who are poor and needy, and thus working to ensure that they participate in God's blessings. This should be true, then, *par excellence*, of our churches. 'Love one another as I have loved you' (John 13:34). Our church communities must, then, be places where those believers who are needy and less well off feel comfortable, accepted, loved and included. Are they?

6. All evangelicals should seek social justice according to their sphere and calling

Not everyone is called to be an evangelist. Not everyone is called to be a Wilberforce or a Shaftesbury. But surely some are. Perhaps we need to pray for God to raise up some to be key workers for social justice in our day.

The call to seek justice, however, is not confined to a few. It is part of God's call to each and every one of us that we become holy and Christlike. Some of us are employed in sen-ior positions in large multinational companies. What are we doing to encourage our businesses to act justly rather than unjustly? It is no good replying that 'business is business'. This last sentence means what it says: such a dictum is no good, that is, it is *not good* – it has nothing to do with a biblical heart or a biblical mind. If we cannot do good in the place where we are working, what on earth are we doing there? In any case, the corporate world is now awash with notions of social responsibility and ethical accountability. We Christians should be at the forefront of those who are able to translate such notions into practical and realistic action.

Some of us have opportunities to encourage social justice in our behaviour as consumers, through the purchase of 'fair trade' products, for example. Others have opportunities in our own local communities to look out and care for those who are poor and in need.

Each of us, then, is to play our part in seeking social justice according to our own calling and sphere of service. As this chapter has argued, the biblical gospel has social justice as a central concern. The challenge for evangelicals is to let this affect our minds, our hearts, our behaviour and our gospel proclamation.

* * *

Revd Dr Andy Hartropp is a church minister and an economist. He is Curate of Christ Church, Watford, and Head of Economics at The Henrietta Barnett School in Hampstead, London. He was formerly Lecturer in Financial Economics at Brunel University.

3

Evangelicals and Contemporary Culture

Luke Bretherton[1]

The Problem: How do Evangelicals relate to contemporary culture?

Some think there is a spectre haunting Evangelicalism – the spectre of dissolution. Labels such as 'unbiblical', 'unsound', 'unedifying' and the like point to the fear that Evangelicalism will be undone unless it can remain distinctive from and find ways of relating to contemporary culture that do not threaten the integrity of evangelical belief and practice (however conceived). Phalanxes of books, articles and conferences are drawn up in battle formation in order to assault the question of how the gospel (the touchstone of evangelical integrity) relates to culture (the ogre that threatens this integrity). From worship to mission to reading the Bible, the relationship between the gospel and culture is seen to affect every area of evangelical belief and practice. Hence the depth of this anxiety: if the relationship is wrong, then every area of evangelical life will be distorted or compromised.

Conversely, others admonish Evangelicals for their 'ghetto mentality' or for being 'withdrawn', 'out of touch' or 'exclusive'. All these accusations turn on exactly the same anxiety as that of those who fear the dissolution of evangelicalism: that is, an anxiety about the proper relationship between Christians and contemporary culture. The fear of dissolution is inverted by those who accuse Evangelicalism of being 'out of touch' and becomes the fear that evangelicals are either exclusive or sectarian or not sufficiently 'engaged with the real issues'.

Debates about the scandal of the evangelical mind, postevangelicalism and the gagging of God all, in one way or another, centre on the question of what is the proper relationship between Evangelicalism and contemporary culture. Is the anxiety about the relationship between Evangelicalism and contemporary culture justified? Should we be worried? I am going to argue that far from being justified, the fears outlined above focus on the wrong thing. More often than not, discussions of the relationship between Evangelicalism and contemporary culture operate with a fallacious picture of the world. Indeed, far from being informed by the Bible or theology, most discussions of this issue are bound by sociological assumptions that are themselves of dubious merit.

Christ and Culture: a False Dichotomy?

The pre-eminent way of thinking about the proper relationship between different forms of Christianity (and I understand Evangelicalism to be a sub-set of Christianity rather than definitive of what it means to be a Christian) and culture has been to analyse them sociologically and develop a typology. Representative of such categorizations, and perhaps the most influential of them, is the typology of Ernst Troeltsch in *The Social Teaching of the Christian Churches*.[2] Troeltsch made a distinction between a 'church' and a 'sect'. The basic difference is that you are born into a 'church' that embraces you, irrespective of your behaviour, but you must actively join a 'sect' and thereafter follow a strict ethical code to remain part of it. Troeltsch observed that theology cannot be separated from sociology. He thought that the 'church' that seeks to embrace everyone will thence proclaim grace. By contrast, an élite 'sect' will stress law. Likewise, the 'church' will affirm the world, whereas the 'sect' will deny the world by retreating from it or attacking it. The 'church' will seek power in the world, and, to achieve it, will make the necessary compromises, whereas the 'sect' will insist on purity and remain at the margins of the world. The 'church' will stress sacraments and education, whereas the 'sect' will emphasize conversion and commitment. Similarly, the respective theology of the 'church' and 'sect' will be different, for their social forms will shape their doctrine. For example, the Christ of a 'church' is a gracious redeemer and the Christ of a 'sect' is a commanding Lord.

A further example of these sociological typologies is that developed by Richard Niebuhr in his influential work *Christ and Culture*.[3] He essentially modified and developed Troeltsch's work. He set out five different types of relation between the 'church' and its neighbours: 'Christ against culture', 'the Christ of culture', 'Christ above culture', 'Christ and culture in paradox' and 'Christ the transformer of culture'. Each of these types expressed both a distinct social formation of Christians and a pattern for how such a formation related to those around it.

Whether consciously or tacitly, most conceptions of the proper way to relate Evangelicalism and contemporary culture follow Troeltsch and Niebuhr. The very framing of this chapter title is an example: on the one side are Evangelicals and on the other is contemporary culture. Framing the title in this way immediately places the emphasis on finding ways of relating the two sides of the equation in order to come up with the right answer. The hallowed ground most often fought over in debates about the relationship between Evangelicalism and culture is the 'Christ the transformer of culture' position, with different sides claiming their approach to culture represents the most transformational position.[4] However, a position shaped by Troeltsch and Niebuhr depends on the 'world' or culture having some autonomous existence that can be set over and against Christ and those who follow him. Among numerous other criticisms of Niebuhr's typology and basic thesis, John Howard Yoder comments:

It is a necessary presupposition of the entire argument that the value of culture is not derived from Jesus Christ but stands somehow independently of him. It is independent of Jesus Christ in the orders of both being and knowing ... Once this axiom is (tacitly) established, then the question will be simply to what extent in particular cases this autonomy is allowed to remain standing over against the call of Jesus, or how it may be qualified.[5]

In sum, Troeltsch and Niebuhr (and those who take a similar approach) establish a false dichotomy between 'Christ' and 'culture'. It is pointless to try and think about the relationship between Evangelicalism (as a particular instance of Christianity) and culture as the relationship between two separate spheres that must be related like circles in a Venn diagram. Christianity and culture are mutually constitutive, inextricably woven together. This is not to say that culture exhausts the meaning and significance of Christian beliefs and practices. Rather, we must call into question the plausibility of clear lines being drawn between any particular group of Christians (e.g. Evangelicals) and their surrounding culture. The dividing line between Christians and non-Christians is more permeable and fluid than conceptions such as Troeltsch's and Niebuhr's allow. More significantly still, both Christianity and culture are constituted and defined by their relationship to their Creator, Lord and Redeemer, Jesus Christ (whether this is acknowledged or not) who, with the Holy Spirit, is at work in both, independently of either. Schemas like Troeltsch's and Niebuhr's limit Christ's sphere of activity to working, in one way or another, through the visible church. However, Christ and the Holy Spirit are at work beyond the bounds of the institutions and social formations we identify as 'church' (in other words, the kingdom of God, while in continuity with the visible church, is not to be wholly equated with it, and may include aspects of any given culture).[6] Moreover, Christ is the very ground of all cultures, their sovereign Judge, and, ultimately, the end they should seek as their fulfilment.

Secularization: a Myth too Far?

A related assumption that underpins many discussions of the relationship between Evangelicalism and culture is what is called the secularization thesis. The secularization thesis assumes that religious affiliation, faith communities and the like decline with the onset of a host of phenomena related to modernity, including urbanization, industrialization, rapid technological change and the increasing influence of the nation state (and its bureaucracy).[7] Unlike the Christ and culture framework, the secularization thesis makes culture not just autonomous, but determinative. Historical forces determine the place of Christianity in the world; thus social, economic and political processes shape the role of the religions rather than vice versa. Questions about the role of Christ and the Spirit in history are never considered.[8] This is rather like focusing on what kind of bread is used at the Eucharist and how it was made in order to determine the meaning and significance of the Eucharist. While such a focus may teach us something about the material conditions of the Christians partaking of that communion service, such a focus can, of itself, reveal nothing about their faith or relationship to God.

The assumption of increasing secularization tends to take two forms in discussions about the relationship between Evangelicalism and contemporary culture. Either it forms the rallying call to resistance (for example, in oft-repeated denunciations of 'secular humanism' in education or the media) or it constitutes a tacit assumption among those who call on Evangelicalism to change in order to make a space for itself in contemporary culture (this is especially true, for example, in debates about mission and worship styles). While these two approaches may look, at first glance, as if they are rejecting or resisting secularization, they accept, albeit tacitly, that the secularization thesis is true and must be countered or adapted to in some way. However, the secularization thesis increasingly looks haggard and frail. Europe, it now appears, is the exception.[9] But even in Europe it is formal attendance at religious services and participation in religious institutions that has declined rather

than the role and significance of the religions *per se*. In other
parts of the world, revival and resurgence abound. The enormous increase of Pentecostalism, notably in Latin America, is an
example of the growing role and significance of the religions,
and Evangelicalism in particular.[10] The issue is not the decline of
religious observance but how religion has adapted to, mirrored
and shaped the contemporary world. Furthermore, the vib-
rancy and growth of Evangelical churches in the contemporary
world and in Britain among black-majority churches suggests
that not only is the secularization thesis conceptually flawed,
but also that its continued use as a guiding assumption serves a
set of vested interests: notably, the interests of white, educated,
Western élites. By letting it inform debates about the relationship between Evangelicalism and contemporary culture we
must ask whose interests are we really serving?

Culture cannot be understood outside of its relations to the *cultus*
– the form of religion and worship – with which it is intrinsically
related, and in the West the predominate *cultus* has been
Christianity. Thus, since all cultures are cultivated from the soil of
a particular *cultus*, culture itself is far from passive or neutral: the
way in which we live our lives affects the way we believe. Yet culture is not coterminous or identical with the *cultus* of Christianity.
The relationship between Evangelicalism and any particular
culture must necessarily be ambiguous, demanding constant
discernment and evaluation. Any given culture may simultaneously direct us to God *and* it may direct us to false gods. It can
increasingly voice creation's praise *and* cause God's good creation
to groan as it awaits redemption (Romans 8:19–23). Any given
culture may both store up treasure that will be brought into the
New Jerusalem at the fulfilment of all things *and* be practising
abomination and falsehood (Revelation 21:26–27).

Where does Bone Begin and Marrow End?

The proper understanding of many aspects of contemporary
culture cannot be understood outside of their relationship to

Evangelicalism. It is foolish to assume Evangelicals are always behind the times, running to catch up with the latest cultural trend. While this may be true in terms of trivial phenomena, it is not true in terms of those trends that substantially shape and inform how we live. From the spawning of suburbia to the advent of the Internet, Evangelicals have either helped shape, or quickly adapted to, many of the dominant features of contemporary culture.

Just as Max Weber realized that Protestantism was a critical influence on the development of capitalism, it should not surprise us that one of its descendents, Evangelicalism, has helped shape contemporary life.[11] Amid a wider thesis that the Enlightenment contained more elements of apparent irrationality and religious enthusiasm, more elements of socially progressive ideas than has been supposed, David Hempton argues that popular Evangelical Christianity collaborated with and exploited Enlightenment ideals of religious toleration in order to further its own development in both Britain and America. He contends also that Evangelicalism was itself a significant factor in the rise of the market economy, the democratization of political culture, the decline of established churches and the slow but perceptible emancipation of women.[12] Similarly, the historian Laurence Moore argues that American religion, of which Evangelicalism is a constitutive part, pioneered many aspects of contemporary consumerism.[13] Another example of how Evangelicals have helped shape contemporary life is how the supposedly 'private' domain of sexuality, the body and gender roles has come to dominate 'public' discourse. The involvement of Evangelicals in debates about issues such as abortion and homosexuality means they have been key participants in the breakdown of this division between the public and private domains. At a more trivial level, it could be argued that the revivalist meetings of late nineteenth- and early twentieth-century Evangelicalism foreshadow and inform the shape of contemporary music concerts. Moody and Sankey rocked stadiums long before Elvis or The Beatles! In his study of Evangelicalism in Britain, David Bebbington concludes:

[Evangelicalism] has shaped the thought-world of a large proportion of the population. It has exerted an immense influence
both on individuals and on the course of social and political
development, particularly in the later nineteenth century. And
it has shown a receptivity that goes some way toward modifying the charge of narrowness... Moulded and remoulded by its
environment, Evangelical religion has been a vital force in
modern Britain.[14]

Where it has not directly shaped contemporary culture,
Evangelicalism has often mirrored or adapted to it. A recent
example of mirroring is the revival of interest in Celtic
Christianity and how this is parallel to a growing interest in
Celtic spirituality among many non-Christians in the West.
Similarly, the growing emphasis on storytelling as a tool for
mission mirrors an increased emphasis on narrative, rather
than didactic forms of learning in education. A more significant relationship may be traced between the emphasis on
subjective, bodily experience among Charismatic Evangelicals
and the emphasis on embodied experience as a criterion of
evaluation (that is, did it make you feel good) in many aspects
of contemporary culture from the New Age movement to the
entertainment industry. One commentator goes so far as to
trace a relationship between the physically ecstatic and eroti-
cized spirituality of much Charismatic worship patterns and
the erotic imagery in which contemporary culture is steeped.[15]
David Lyon argues that phenomena such as the Toronto
Blessing mirror patterns of what he calls 'glocalization'; that is,
globalized phenomena that depend on modern communication technology and travel for transmission, yet take diverse
and locally flavoured forms.[16] The Alpha course could be seen
in the same light.

We are not claiming that the ability of Evangelicalism to
shape or adapt to its environment is always a good thing. For
example, its adaptability can easily mutate into a quest for relevance or a search to find the right technique to connect to a
presumed to be 'secular' audience. For example, the music
arranger at the Axis Church (an offshoot of Willow Creek, a

large and growing church and church network in the USA) states: 'We pick songs right off the radio. The most important thing in the music we pick is relevancy... We try to keep it familiar.'[17] The quest for relevance and the right 'evangelistic' tool or technique are symptomatic of many church growth strategies. In essence, such approaches to proclaiming the gospel sever the link between belief and practice such that effectiveness (rather than theology or the Bible) becomes the primary criteria for determining whether something is worthwhile or not. This is the worst kind of adapting to contemporary culture possible: it makes bureaucratic rationality and the tyranny of the present, rather than the actions of Christ and the Spirit and the wisdom of our forebears, the primary influence on belief and practice.

Our primary concern is to say that the sociologically defined influence or otherwise of Evangelicalism on contemporary culture can tell us next to nothing about the worth or righteousness of the relationship between Evangelicalism and contemporary culture. The worth of this relationship can only be evaluated by discerning the degree to which Evangelicalism constitutes a faithful witness to the life, death and resurrection of Jesus Christ, and how far its relationship with its friends, enemies and indifferent neighbours in the contemporary culture promotes or detracts from such witness.

The Break between Belief and Practice

It is at the point where we must discern how to evaluate whether Evangelical thought and practice bear faithful witness to Jesus Christ that questions about how our communities nurture and enable us to see and hear 'Christianly' come into view.[18] And it is at this point that we encounter perhaps the key problem of Evangelicalism in contemporary culture: that is, the break between belief and practice so that our churches cease to be communities of nurture and become no more than playgrounds of experience, undisciplined by either reflection on the Bible or the wisdom of our elders (be they John Stott or

John Chrysostom). The problem is the increasing fissure between belief and practice; hence ways in which Evangelicals are like and unlike their culture are unconditioned and undisciplined by theological frameworks of meaning. It is precisely this fear of the break between belief and practice that seems to haunt Alister McGrath's prodigious efforts to reinvigorate the intellectual resources of Evangelicals.[19]

Hospitality and holiness

In an attempt to address this issue of the break between belief and practice, with regard to the relationship between Evangelicalism and contemporary culture, I propose to analyse this relationship through examining the tension between hospitality and holiness that occurs time and again in Scripture. This would seem to be a far more 'biblical' way of thinking about the issues under discussion than conceiving of the relationship either as one determined solely by historical forces or where the relationship is thought of as a battle between two opposing sides.

Hospitality and holiness are central themes in Jesus' ministry. The images of hospitality are abundant and vivid. Among many, there are: the wedding at Cana; the rich man feasting while Lazarus starves at his gate; the joyous meal at Jericho with Zacchaeus; the woman washing Jesus' feet; Jesus washing his disciples' feet; the Last Supper; and the meals enjoyed with the risen Jesus. As N.T. Wright points out, 'Most writers now agree that eating with "sinners" was one of the most characteristic and striking marks of Jesus' regular activity.'[20] Yet at the same time, in both his teaching and by example, Jesus constantly emphasizes the need for holiness.

There is both continuity with and departure from the Old Testament in the pattern of hospitality and the call to holiness Jesus establishes. In the Old Testament God commanded His people to provide hospitality to strangers: 'The alien who resides with you shall be to you as the citizen among you; you shall love the alien as yourself, for you were aliens in the land of Egypt: I am the Lord your God' (Leviticus 19:33–34). The

command of Leviticus 19 was echoed in a range of other legis-
lation. The tithe, for instance, is fundamentally a command to
be hospitable on a lavish scale (Deuteronomy 12:17–19).
Again, the commands concerning harvesting are demands
that hospitality be observed: one who harvests a field must not
seek to maximize his harvest, but must leave the gleanings for
those who are in need (Deuteronomy 24:19–22). Stories of hospitality constitute a leitmotif throughout the Old Testament:
for example, Abraham and Sarah entertaining angels (Genesis
18); Abigail placating David (1 Samuel 25); and the widow of
Zarephath caring for Elijah (1 Kings 17:18–24). At times this
hospitality is not only offered but also demanded, as when Lot
insists that the angels spend the night with him (Genesis
19:1–3). At others times it is extended to enemies as a sign of
the reconciling work of God, as when Isaac made a feast for
Abimelech (Genesis 26:26–31), or Elisha mediated a peace
between the Arameans and the Israelites (2 Kings 6:8–23). It is
linked with the renewal of creation (Ecclesiastes 10:16–17), and
ultimately it comes to include all creation and all the nations at
the messianic banquet, as depicted and anticipated in the
prophets (Isaiah 25, 54; Ezekiel 39; Joel 2 – 3). Jesus' ministry
draws together all these elements, intensifies their application
and inaugurates their fulfilment.

Alongside this emphasis on hospitality there is the call for
holiness. There is much in the Old Testament that emphasizes
how Israel is not to entertain its neighbours or have contact with
those who are unclean. There are the numerous purity rituals
set out in the Torah,[21] and, most significantly, we cannot ignore
all the material relating to the conquest of those already living
in Canaan in Joshua and elsewhere. There is also the connection
between being faithless to God and marrying foreign women,
expressed in Joshua, Ezra and Nehemiah (Joshua 23:11–13; Ezra
10:2–4, 10:10; Nehemiah 13:26–27). It seems Israel is constantly
in danger of being overwhelmed by pollution and sin (the two
being distinct) and must constantly protect itself in order to
maintain itself as holy and distinct among the nations.

Jesus does not resolve the tension between hospitality and
holiness present in the Old Testament, but he does relate

these two imperatives in a particular way. Jesus relates hospitality and holiness by inverting their relations: hospitality becomes the means of holiness. Instead of having to be set apart from or exclude pagans in order to maintain holiness, it is in Jesus' hospitality towards pagans, the unclean and sinners that His own holiness is shown. Instead of sin and impurity infecting Him, it seems Jesus' purity and righteousness somehow 'infects' the impure, sinners and the Gentiles. For example, the haemorrhaging woman has only to touch Jesus and she is healed and made clean (Mark 5:25–34; Luke 8:43–48). Instead of Jesus having to undergo purity rituals because of contact with the woman, as any other rabbi would, it is the woman who is 'cleansed' by contact with Him. There is a similar dynamic when Jesus touches lepers, the dead, the blind, the deaf and dumb, or partakes of a meal with a tax collector.

Jesus' speech and action announces a form of hospitality that, to some of His contemporaries, is shocking in relation to certain Old Testament precedents. Thus His hospitality brings Him into conflict with the custodians of Israel's purity, both self-appointed (the Pharisees, Zealots and so on) and actual (the Temple authorities). Some scholars contend that this conflict between Jesus and His contemporaries is about the shape and purpose of the people of God, which is itself part of a wider debate about the response of Judaism to Roman political power and the encroachment of Hellenistic culture,[22] a debate that has its analogue in the arguments that exist today around the issue of the relationship between Evangelicalism and contemporary culture. Through His hospitality Jesus rejected and presented an alternative to every other post-exilic programme for Israel's internal reform and quest for holiness, for all of these were based on the exclusion of 'sinners', separation from the 'world' (that is, Gentile uncleanness and rule), and solidarity formed by defining Israel's identity through opposition to sinners and Gentiles. Jesus also rejected co-option by and assimilation with the dominant pagan social order and capitulation to sin. Rather, He advocated participation in the kingdom of God as enacted in His table fellowship. Jesus' hospitality is not to be isolated to Himself: He calls His disciples to 'Go and do likewise' (Luke10:37).

The tension between the imperative of hospitality to strangers and the call to holiness has to be renegotiated in each cultural context as different questions about what to affirm and what to stand against, who to welcome and who to reject, occur.[23] However, it is following after and bearing witness to the pattern established by Jesus Christ that determines how to do this, and it is the Holy Spirit who empowers us to do this.

Framing the problem of how Evangelicals relate with their neighbours in contemporary culture in terms of the tension between hospitality and holiness helps bring into focus what lies at the heart of this tension; that is, the way in which being a Christian marks one off as distinctive by one's belief and practice from one's neighbours. However, the nature of this distinctiveness is peculiar and often misconstrued.

Eschatological distinctiveness

Prior to conversion, a Christian might be similar to, or distinct from, their neighbour at any level of identity. After conversion, any similarity or difference is called into question since ethnic, familial, political and all other identities are relativized. A new distance arises between the Christian and non-Christian, hence the biblical leitmotif of Christians being 'aliens' and 'sojourners'. The metaphor 'sojourner' or '*perigrinus*' is a powerful one because it sums up central themes from Scripture and expresses some fundamental perspectives about the problem of the identity and difference of the people of God from their neighbours. This sense of being a stranger is perhaps best expressed in the term 'pilgrim'. Augustine summarizes the implications of this as follows:

> The Church proceeds, a pilgrim, in these evil days, not merely since the time of the bodily presence of Christ and his apostles, but since Abel himself, the first righteous man, whom his impious brother killed, and from then on until the end of time, among the persecutions of the world, and the consolations of God.[24]

The difference between Christians and non-Christians is at heart an eschatological one. God breaks into the midst of the world in which Christians live with a new home, the dimensions and nature of which will be made fully manifest at the fulfilment of time. New birth commences the journey to this new home. However, the journey does not lead away from where they live: it leads them to the epicentre of their former home, for the house of God, although distinct from the world, is bursting the bounds of, and being erected in the midst of, their old home. The church is distinct from its culture, yet it belongs to its culture: it is in the world but not of the world. As at Pentecost, the differences of indigenous cultures are not erased but reconfigured into a unity given of the Spirit.[25] Differentiation and distance from where we 'belong', or what determines our identity, no longer requires an actual geographic move, as it did for Abraham and the Israelites in Egypt, nor a cultural separation either from society, as it did for the Essenes, or within society, as the Pharisees proposed. Neither does it involve building a new home through force of arms and the practice of politics shaped by the 'principalities and powers' as it did for the Zealots, nor the erasing of all existing patterns and traditions of social life in order to start afresh, as various utopians have demanded. Lastly, it does not involve simply performing the right rituals and saying the right words, while settling for the status quo, as it did for the Sadducees. Rather, it is only through Jesus Christ that we are born again *in* the midst of and not *from* the midst of a culture. In other words, being good, pure, holy and moral cannot be secured either by withdrawal from, assimilation to, or the destruction of our culture. Hence, we must neither deny our cultural inheritance nor over-freight it with significance. Neither can we deny the cultural inheritance of others nor over-freight another's culture with significance. The Christian cannot turn against his or her cultural background in self-hatred; neither can he or she revel in it as the apogee of civilization. Instead, as someone who has been through the death and new birth of baptism and thus participates in the resurrection life of Jesus Christ, the Christian finds himself or herself in a relation with his or her neighbours of both distance and belonging. There is much we can affirm and participate in the life of our friends and neighbours, and there is much we must bear witness against. The simultaneous distance from and belonging to their culture that Christians experience is a feature of life between this age and the next, between the inauguration of God's kingdom and its full disclosure when Christ returns.

Relations between Christians and non-Christians must account for this eschatological distinctiveness. As Miroslav Volf points out:

> Christians do not come into their social world from outside seeking either to accommodate to their new home (like second generation immigrants would), shape it in the image of the one they have left behind (like colonizers would), or establish a little haven in the strange new world reminiscent of the old (as resident aliens would). They are not outsiders who either seek to become insiders or maintain strenuously the status of outsiders ... Christian difference is therefore not an insertion of something new into the old from outside, but a bursting out of the new *precisely within the proper space of the old*.[26]

The church does not become a 'culture' in and of itself; hence it is not one culture among many. Instead, the church and its practices are the paradigmatic signs of a given culture's redemption through the sacrifice and priesthood of Jesus Christ. The church is to be a people invested with the character of the gospel, which is simultaneously to bear witness to how a given culture may be eschatologically fulfilled. Therefore, in this age, no clear dividing lines can be identified between Christians and non-Christians: all such division will only become clear on judgement day. There can be no strongly delineated clash of civilizations or culture wars; rather, questions about what to reject and what to retain confront Christians constantly as they participate in and bear witness to God's transfiguration of their culture.[27] The criteria for deciding about what to reject and what to accept is straightforward if not always clear: that is, we must ask of what we do, or what our neighbours are doing, does it bear witness, in any shape or form, to the life, death and resurrection of Jesus Christ?

Scripture testifies to how God's action draws a multiplicity of cultures into a single salvation history and elects a particular people whose life together, while specific and particular, is constituted by the transfiguring of other cultures. Perhaps the most significant example of this transfiguring process at work is David's act of using a city (created by Cain and, as Augustine and others have argued, the paradigmatic embodiment of human alienation from God), and moreover, a pagan city, Jebus, as the basis of Jerusalem, a place where God's glory resided (1 Chronicles 11:3–8; Ezekiel 16).[28] To use a picture from the New Testament, the water from stone jars becomes the wine at the wedding feast through the transfiguring actions of Christ and the Spirit.

Conclusion

I have tried to distinguish a properly theological way of thinking about the relationship between Evangelical Christians and contemporary culture, one not conditioned by false assumptions about the way the world is. One false assumption that sadly often frames discussion of the relationship between Evangelicalism and culture is the assumption that culture is some kind of autonomous sphere, with a life of its own, that Christians must build bridges to or erect walls against. Another wrong assumption takes the form of the secularization thesis: this assumes that culture and historical forces determine the place of the religions and ignores the ways in which Christianity and culture are mutually constitutive. In place of these wrong assumptions I have proposed a theologically derived framework for thinking about the relationship between Evangelicals and their neighbours. I argued that the call to hospitality and holiness and the eschatological nature of Christian distinctiveness should shape how we understand the situation of Evangelicals today. In short, Evangelicals are both like and unlike their neighbours and the criteria to discern in what ways their distinctiveness is good and in what ways it is bad must be determined by whether or not the life of Evangelicals and the life of their neighbours testifies to the evangel – the good news that Christ has died, Christ has risen and Christ will come again. How to do this is another question altogether![29]

* * *

Dr Luke Bretherton teaches at the South East Institute for Theological Education, training Anglican, Methodist and URC candidates for ordination. His doctorate, in moral theology and philosophy, is from King's College, London, where he also taught the Christian Ethics MA. He has previously worked for CARE, the Bible Society and the St Ethelburga's Centre for Reconciliation and Peace.

Notes

1 I am greatly indebted to Sára Miklós, Nick Townsend and Herb Schlossberg for all their helpful criticisms of earlier drafts. The errors and mistakes, however, are all mine.

2 Ernst Troeltsch, *The Social Teaching of the Christian Churches*, Olive Wyon (tr.) 2 vols (London: George Allen & Unwin, 1931).

3 Richard Niebuhr, *Christ and Culture* (London: Faber & Faber, 1952).

4 The very title of the *Transformation Journal*, an Evangelical publication that focuses on mission and ethics, is indicative of such an aspiration.

5 John Howard Yoder, 'How H. Richard Niebuhr Reasoned: A Critique of *Christ and Culture*' in *Authentic Transformation: A New Vision of Christ and Culture*, Glen H. Stassen, John H. Yoder and D.M. Yeager (eds) (Nashville: Abingdon, 1996), pp. 31–90 (above quote on p. 55).

6 This point is of crucial importance. As Augustine and others argue, the visible church is the contingent and fallen form of the invisible church, which forms the truly human society in this age.

The church is not to be overequated with the coming kingdom of God. To do so would be to fall into a prematurely realized eschatology wherein two fallacies are legitimized: first, the fallacy that the more the visible church increases the more the glory of God is seen (i.e. the stronger and bigger the church the better); second, the fallacy that if the growth of the church makes the glory of God more visible then everything must be made to serve the increase of the church (i.e. effectiveness rather than faithfulness is what counts).

Douglas Farrow argues that a better insurance against the over-identification of a particular sociological and institutional pattern with the true church is to emphasize the humanity of the ascended Christ and not the wheat and tares character of the visible church. If the continued humanity of the ascended Christ is emphasized then no church can claim purity in its own life, for its purity is dependent on its restored humanity in Christ through the Spirit. Furthermore, it is not the role of the church to create and build the kingdom. Rather, it is the role of church to bear witness in its life together to the kingdom as it is becoming here and now through the actions of Christ in the Spirit. See Douglas Farrow, *Ascension and Ecclesia: On the Significance of the Doctrine of the Ascension for Ecclesiology and Christian Cosmology* (Edinburgh: T&T Clark, 1999), pp. 121–9.

7 For a definition and a full critique of the secularization thesis, see David Lyon, *Jesus in Disneyland* (Oxford: Polity Press, 2000), pp. 22–35. See also, Lesslie Newbigin, *The Gospel in a Pluralist Society* (London: SPCK, 1989), pp. 211–21.

8 For a thorough theological critique of sociology and how it inherently excludes theological criteria of evaluation see John Milbank, *Theology and Social Theory: Beyond Secular Reason* (Oxford: Basil Blackwell, 1990).

9 Grace Davie, 'Europe: The Exception That Proves the Rule' in, Peter Berger (ed.) *The Impact of Religious Conviction on the Politics of the Twenty-first Century* (Grand Rapids: Eerdmans, 1999), ch. 6.

10 See, for example, David Martin, *Tongues of Fire: The Explosion of Protestantism in Latin America* (Oxford: Blackwell, 1990).

11 Max Weber, *The Protestant Ethic and the Spirit of Capitalism* (London: Allen & Unwin, 1976).

12 David Hempton, 'Enlightenment and Enthusiasm: Popular Christianity in Trans-Atlantic Perspective, 1750–2000' (Maurice Lectures, King's College, London, April 2000).

13 Laurence Moore, *Selling God: American Religion in the Marketplace of Culture* (Oxford: Oxford University Press, 1994).

14 David Bebbington, *Evangelicalism in Modern Britain: A History from the 1730s to the 1980s* (London and New York: Routledge, 1989), p. 276.

15 Martyn Percy, 'Sweet Rapture: Subliminal Eroticism in Postmodern Charismatic Worship' in *Theology and the Body: Gender, Text and Ideology*, R. Hannaford and J. Jobling (eds) (Herefordshire: Gracewing, 1999), pp. 1–29.

16 Lyon, *Jesus in Disneyland*, pp. 106–13. The paradigm example of this is the McDonald's lamb burger sold in India.

17 Quoted from Karen Beattie, 'Meeting at the "Axis"', *Re:generation Quarterly* vol. 3.1, 1997, p. 31.

18 On this see Stanley Hauerwas, *The Peaceable Kingdom: A Primer in Christian Ethics* (Notre Dame: University of Notre Dame Press, 1983) or Stanley Hauerwas and William H. Willimon, *Resident Aliens: Life in the Christian Colony* (Nashville: Abingdon, 1989).

19 See, for example, Alister McGrath, *Evangelicalism and the Future of Christianity* (London: Hodder & Stoughton, 1988).

20 N.T. Wright, *Jesus and the Victory of God: Christian Origins and the Question of God* (London: SPCK, 1996), p. 431.

21 For an assessment of the relationship between Israel's holiness, the Temple cult and Israel's distinctive identity in relation to other nations, see Jacob Milgrom, *Leviticus 1–16*, 3 vols, *Anchor Bible* (New York: Doubleday, 1991), vol. 3.

22 For example, see Marcus Borg, *Conflict, Holiness and Politics in the Teachings of Jesus* (Lampeter: Edwin Mellen Press, 1972), pp. 2–4.

23 For examples of how this process took place in the transition from the late Roman empire to the early medieval era, see R.A. Markus, *The End of Ancient Christianity* (Cambridge: Cambridge University Press, 1990).

24 Augustine, *City of God* 18.51, translated by Gerard O'Daly in *Augustine's City of God: A Reader's Guide* (Oxford: Clarendon Press, 1999), p. 159.

25 See Michael Welker, *God the Spirit*, John Hoffmeyer (tr.) (Minneapolis: Fortress Press, 1992), pp. 232–3.

26 Miroslav Volf, 'Soft Difference: Theological Reflections on the Relation Between Church and Culture in 1 Peter', *Ex Auditu* 10 (1994), pp. 15–30 (above quote on pp. 18–19).

27 The point of distinction with Niebuhr here is that it is God who does the transforming, not the church. The role of the church is to testify to the actions of God in history.

28 See also Jacques Ellul, *The Meaning of the City* (Carlisle: Paternoster Press, 1997), pp. 94–7.

29 It does at times seem as if the debate among Christians (and Evangelicals in particular) about how to interpret and live out the pattern of Christ's life, death and resurrection is interminable and that we can never be certain that 'our' way is the best way. However, we should always remember that 'certainty' is a subjective, psychological condition rather than an epistemological category. Alongside a host of other spiritual disciplines, it is through debating about how to interpret the pattern of Christ's life, death and resurrection in relation to any particular issue, and debating it both with our peers and with our elders like Irenaeus, Calvin, Wesley etc., and in learning faithful patterns of debate (just, generous, peaceable and rigorous conversation), that we grow in the wisdom, virtue and confidence that enables us to become the kinds of people who can bear faithful witness to Jesus Christ.

4

Evangelicals and the Human Person

David Jackman

By definition, to be evangelical is all about the gospel. To be evangelical is to believe that the good news is that Jesus Christ is our Lord, and to proclaim Him to others so that they also will believe and be saved. Evangelism constitutes a significant part of our duty both to God and to our fellow human beings. With regard to God, it is firstly an expression of praise and gratitude for his delivering grace, and secondly a response of obedience to the commission of the risen Christ. Evangelism declares in word and action that Jesus Christ is both our rescuer and our ruler. With regard to others, it is an act of love presenting the only message that can generate faith, so as to rescue men and women from God's righteous wrath against our sinful rebellion and its inevitable consequence in hell. 'Are you saved?' was the urgent question often on the lips of a past generation, and while it is rarely heard in that form of words today, that is still the heartbeat of healthy, biblical evangelical Christianity today.

But what does it mean 'to be saved'? Clearly, the fundamental idea is that of rescue from great danger, probably life-threatening in its seriousness. The New Testament leaves us in no doubt that God's righteous wrath is already being revealed against all human godlessness and wickedness, and that at the last day, when Christ brings in His eternal kingdom, God's perfect justice will implement His sentence of punishment and separation on all the unrepentant. Being saved therefore has a strong future focus in Scripture. On the day when 'men will flee to caves in the rocks and to holes in the ground from the dread of the Lord and the splendour of his majesty' (Isaiah 2:19) we shall know just how great that salvation really is. But if salvation is focused on God's coming in judgement on the future 'day of the Lord', it also stretches beyond that critical moment on into eternity and the biblical vision of heaven. We are saved from wrath for heaven, or 'glory', as it is sometimes termed. Transformed into the likeness of Christ and with Him forever in His eternal kingdom, the Christian looks forward with eager expectation to the experience of unhindered fellowship with God. When the stakes are this high, it is hardly surprising that evangelical Christians should be passionate about the priority of evangelism.

However, a number of questions immediately emerge. If the predominant emphasis of the New Testament teaching on salvation is eschatological, focused on the end of time, what are the present implications of the gospel? How should the Christian view his or her life on planet earth? 'All men are like grass and all their glory is like the flowers of the field', says Isaiah (40:6). James compares human life to a fast-vanishing mist (James 4:14), while Peter sees the whole planet as destined for God's destroying fire (2 Peter 3:7). So what value or purpose does life in this world have? What on earth are we here for?

Evangelicals have sometimes answered such questions entirely with reference to the eternal future. In short, we are here to 'snatch the brands from the burning', to spread the gospel, and by devotion to that primary task, to seek to win as many as possible for the eternal kingdom. I would not want to disparage that view in any way. It clearly represents a major strand of New Testament teaching and in many current 'Evangelical' circles urgently needs to be re-emphasized. The danger comes when life begins to be defined exclusively in terms of evangelism, and a mechanistic, reductionist attitude takes over. The irony is that this is almost always counterproductive evangelistically. People begin to be seen exclusively as 'souls to be saved' rather than whole persons to be loved and valued. Daily work becomes an increasingly irksome and frustrating (though necessary) interlude between bouts of what really matters, but without any real significance or goal. Human relationships always have an evangelistic, utilitarian purpose, so that individuals are picked up and dropped according to their perceived response. I am speaking about the extreme end of a spectrum, in order to clarify my point. Such attitudes are by no means confined to ardent Christians, I know, but the tendency is plain and its unchecked development can be tragic.

Such attitudes are at odds with the way the New Testament looks at the 'normal' Christian life in the world. It is an interesting fact that its pages are not liberally sprinkled with exhortations to live exclusively for evangelism, though clearly the great commission governs every true Christian's priorities and programme. We are to live for Christ and the gospel. The issue is how to do that, while the danger is that we take part of the biblical answer and regard it as the whole. In the passage in 2 Peter, referred to earlier, this very question is posed. The answer is both ordinary and hugely demanding: 'You ought to live holy and godly lives … make every effort to be found spotless, blameless and at peace with him' (2 Peter 3:14). Far from the future perspective rendering life in this world meaningless, or without lasting significance, it dignifies and deepens our understanding of what it is to be human beings, living in a right relationship with our creator. Nor is this an exclusive emphasis in Peter. It has been calculated that the second coming of Christ is mentioned, on average, once in every thirteen verses of the New Testament, but the applicatory significance is almost exclusively moral and ethical. So, as Christians live these days in the light of that great day that is coming, they do not become 'so heavenly minded that they are no earthly use', to quote the old tag. Quite the opposite. The mark of real godliness is a greater commitment to a fully human life in this world, while recognizing all the time that our true citizenship is in a heavenly city, so that we will always be strangers and aliens, pilgrims, not settlers.

In order to see how rooted this concept is in the whole Biblical revelation, we need to take a brief theological overview, starting in Genesis. 'So God created man in his own image, in the image of God he created him; male and female he created them' (Genesis 1:27). Clearly, humanity derives its distinctiveness in the whole created order from the image, or likeness, of God implanted in our creation. Among many other implications of this statement are the innate human abilities to think with objectivity and self-awareness, to choose how to act, and to love and to worship, especially in relationship to the Creator Himself. Human life in this world derives all its ultimate value and significance from the God who made both. Nor should we forget that at the end of the creation narrative we are told 'God saw all that he had made, and it was very good' (Genesis 1:31). Human life is God's idea and a very good idea too. We need to remember this because when we consider the depths of moral degradation to which we humans sink in our sinful rebellion against God, we can sometimes develop an anti-human way of thinking, which is thoroughly negative and ungodly.

The entrance of sin into the world, in the historical event of the Fall, changes and forever afterwards (at least in time, but not in eternity) distorts and defaces God's good creation purposes. Human beings no longer relate to God or to one another as originally intended by the Creator. Even their relationship to the physical environment is radically altered. In every generation since, the family likeness as 'sons of Adam and daughters of Eve', in C.S. Lewis's phrase, has been undeniably demonstrated. We sin habitually because we are born sinners, and because we are sinners, we go on sinning. The image of God in us is thereby spoiled and marred, but not entirely eradicated. Sometimes referred to as God's 'common grace', it is clear that human beings are not as wicked as they possibly could be, because of God's restraining hand and because of the vestiges of His image in all. Conscience is a further evidence of this. So while the Bible teaches that no part of the human personality or experience is unaffected by the ravages of our sin ('total depravity'), it also affirms that the image of God is residually revealed in acts of love and compassion, in marriage and family life, in caring for the disadvantaged and oppressed. These are never works of righteousness by which we can make ourselves acceptable to God, for then the gospel would be redundant. But they are signs that, in spite of the Fall, God has not given up on the creatures made in His image.

Indeed, that note of hope dominates the rest of the Old Testament story. It is the record of the Creator's grace, moving out in saving mercy, to give His rebellious creatures what they do not deserve, and not to give them what they do. So Noah found grace in the eyes of the Lord, and as a result was declared righteous and rescued from the flood by God's provision of the ark. Abraham received the covenant promise of blessing through his seed coming to all the nations of the world and, in believing God, it was credited to him as righteousness. Eventually, the sons of Jacob are delivered from slavery in Egypt and constituted as the nation of Israel, 'my firstborn son' (Exodus 4:22). Brought to Mount Sinai, they are now face to face with God, their Creator and now their Redeemer, who gives them His divine instruction (Torah) to teach them how to live in this world as His own special people. But then the whole sad story of Israel's persistent failure and rebellion unfolds down the succeeding centuries, until it becomes clear that the infection of sin in Adam's descendants will never be able to be eradicated. There will have to be a new start, a new birth, as it were, with a second Adam to become the head of a new humanity. He will be none other than Emmanuel – God with us – for only a mighty divine intervention will be sufficient to bring fallen human beings back into a right relationship with God; to restore the image of God in humanity and to regain all that was lost in Eden. So the concept of the Messiah, God's chosen one, the anointed King and the suffering Servant, eventually came to its fulfilment in Bethlehem, when Jesus was born as rescuer and ruler.

With the entry of God into time and space history and His clothing Himself in our humanity, we now have a perfect picture of what the image of God in human beings should look like. The gospels are full of practical help to understand what 'holy and godly lives' will look like in this world. Christ's perfect love for the Father is revealed in His total obedience to fulfil the law and accomplish His will. That love is mirrored in all his interpersonal human relationships, whether seen in his compassion for the lost, his anger at religious hypocrisy or his equipping of his disciples. While it is undoubtedly true that He came to earth to die, as God's sacrificial Lamb, for the sins of the whole world, it is equally true that His earthly life of perfection provided us all with the definitive masterclass in what it means to be a human being. Moreover, it was precisely because He always fulfilled the Father's will that He was able to offer His sinless human will as the atoning sacrifice for our sinful, rebellious wills when He gave up His life on the cross. It is no surprise, then, to find that a proper response to Christ is to repent and believe the good news, and then to live as Jesus did, in this world. 'He himself bore our sins in his body on the tree, so that we might die to sins and live for righteousness' (1 Peter 2:24).

At the heart of the gospel of Christ, then, lies nothing less than restoration of the full image of God in every individual who turns to Him and trusts His work. This is the ultimate answer to how the gospel impacts our humanity, our lives in this world, and it is the logical consequence of God's purposes of grace sweeping through the whole flow of Scripture from the Garden of Eden to the City of Gold, the new Jerusalem. The new birth, when we repent and believe the good news, sees the very life of God implanted in the souls of ordinary sinful men and women, such as we are. This is described as the indwelling ministry of the Holy Spirit, given to every believing Christian in order to bring the life of Jesus in His risen power into our everyday experience. Another way of describing the same reality, frequently used by the apostle Paul, is to describe the Christian as being 'in Christ', indissolubly joined to Him by faith, so that Christ lives in His people and His people live in Him. This is the restoration of our true humanity.

There is one other important theological strand that our union with Christ draws in, and which is essential, though frequently overlooked, for our understanding of Christian personhood. In Romans 6, for example, being 'in Christ' is closely related to sharing in the benefits of His cross and resurrection. We are comparatively familiar with the idea of Christ's death dealing with the problem of our sin, and much gospel proclamation focuses on that. But do we understand and proclaim the benefits of the resurrection as centrally as the apostles did? Contemporary 'Evangelicals' often major on the evidentialist apologetic of the empty tomb, but more needs to be said about the personal significance of Christ's resurrection for us as human beings. This is where Paul's magisterial argument in 1 Corinthians 15 is such a help. Taking the analogy of Christ as 'the last Adam', he develops the idea that he is the representative head of a new order of humanity, of which Christ is Himself 'the firstfruits'. This image is not only temporal but qualitative. Firstfruits are the forerunner of the harvest but are of the same appearance and substance as that which will come later. 'And just as we have borne the likeness of the earthly man, so shall we bear the likeness of the man from heaven.' That is the end point of salvation, which clearly must have profound significance for the present. The 'not yet' of heaven dictates the 'now' of earth. Human life is thus dignified with eternal significance and given its focus for godliness. It is the adventure of growing into the likeness of Christ and of the image of God being progressively restored, albeit slowly and with many reverses. For the reality of the gospel is that it transforms our experience of personhood and establishes us on the pathway that will only end at the throne of God. As Paul put it, 'We are being transformed into his likeness with ever-increasing glory, which comes from the Lord, who is the Spirit' (2 Corinthians 3:18). Nothing less is adequate as God's agenda for life in this present world. He wants us to be more like the Lord Jesus.

I have spent time on these biblical roots since they seem today so often to be unknown, or ignored, leading to the sort of mechanistic reductionism that is a travesty of full-orbed New Testament Christianity. This lies behind our slide into legalism and activism as well as the comparatively low expectations of growth in Christlikeness that beset contemporary

'Evangelicalism'. It is time now to explore the implications of this high view that Scripture has of our humanness and to seek to highlight areas of need and concern in contemporary application.

Since the gospel does not negate but transforms our humanity, by restoring the good which God intended in His original act of creation, we cannot ignore any aspect of our true selves or our lives in God's world. Where Christ is Lord every part of our being is subject to His control. Yet it is common for Christian people either to switch off their minds and simply respond intuitively to what they think is God's will, or to deny their feelings and retreat into an exclusively cerebral form of intellectualist faith. In either case, the end product is far less human than God intends us to be. Our starting point in application must be the realization that Christianity is all about a God to be known, loved and worshipped, in the person of the Lord Jesus Christ. 'I want to know Christ' was the apostle Paul's dominating ambition, reminding us that while biblical truth is, of course, propositional, it is also relational. Scripture is primarily God's urgent and gracious revelation of Himself, which summons us into a living relationship with Him, before it is a set of doctrines or a code of conduct. It provides both, but only derivatively from the true knowledge of God, which comes through a personally active response to the written revelation and a resulting, vital relationship with Him. Knowing about God is never a substitute for knowing God personally.

The Christ whom we come to know in the gospel continues in His resurrected, glorified body in heaven to be both fully divine and fully human. On earth, He shared the common lot of human beings. He knew pain and fear, hunger and tiredness, disappointment and elation, sorrow and joy, temptation and victory, suffering, death and resurrection. He had fully to share the whole gamut of our human experience if He was to be able to act as our sin bearer and mediator. It was therefore no part of Christ's earthly life and ministry to deny any aspect of being fully human, but for all that complex creation to be submitted to the Father's revealed character and obedient to the Father's express will. He experienced childhood and adolescence, family life and community living, friendship and fellowship, including the pain of betrayal. None of our challenges or pressure points are outside the range of His experience. We can never say that He doesn't know how we feel. Jesus knows all about our human struggles – from the inside. But empathy is not His greatest gift. Rather it is His unfailing application of divine truth to all the changing scenes of life that provides such a masterclass in what it is to be a truly human being and such an example of godly living for us to follow.

That is a test for what it means to be truly evangelical in our increasingly hedonistic, materialist culture. Over a century ago, the German philosopher Friedrich Nietzsche is reported to have said that he would not consider becoming a Christian until Christ's followers looked a lot more like their Lord. He did not, and we are still coping with the fall-out of his egocentric godlessness. But the challenge is still there. In an age where the very concept of absolute truth is scorned, the way under the radar screen is still supremely the quality of the love and life of Christ revealed in His people. Most people come to faith initially by seeing Christ in the life of one of His followers and then by meeting Him in His word. It is a wonderful strategy, of which His own incarnation is the epitome. But while the Word was 'made flesh', once and for all, uniquely, in the person of Jesus of Nazareth, it is also true that God's plan is to 'flesh out' the truth of that Word through the lives of every one of His believing people. The unique perspective that God's revelation, through the living Word and the written word, can give to all the dilemmas of our humanness is arguably the greatest tool for evangelism through godly living that we have, or could need. Yet often 'Evangelical' churches and believers seem to present at best a slightly Christianized version of the wisdom of our cultural prejudices rather than a radically countercultural alternative. In areas like self-worth, marriage and singleness, parenting, depression, even church management and growth or spiritual leadership, much of the advice and resources available bear very little difference from the self-help sections in the secular bookshop. The wisdom of the world not only goes unchallenged, but is reflected and even aped by a Christianity that sees Jesus as an extra ingredient, a 'spiritual plus', to a life almost indistinguishable from the norms of the cultural context all around us. Let us take a few examples.

Everybody is looking for meaningful, satisfying relationships. This is part of what it means to be made in God's image, as we have seen. The God of the Bible is revealed as the Trinity, in which the three persons constantly interact with one another in dynamic relationships of love. Thus Scripture can teach us not just that God loves, but that God is love. This is the essential unity of God, preserved and demonstrated in the diversity of role of each of the three persons. Christians ought therefore to be the world's leading exponents of dynamic loving relationships, both within their church fellowships, and in their relating to those who do not yet know God. Society is full of desperately lonely and often insecure people, whose motto in life is that you cannot trust anyone and whose view of loving relationships is soured and sometimes just plain cynical. Why are they not flocking to our churches to find what they so much lack? Because within those churches you will find many lonely people with exactly the same needs, even though they are Christians. Their unmet needs mean that they are still in 'demand mode' and unable to meet the needs of others. Instead of the godly love that bears one another's burdens, they find a superficial 'mateyness' that would prefer not to get involved. The two- or three-minute regulation 'say hello to your neighbour' time during the service can so easily stand in for any in-depth care or concern. It keeps everything at the arm's-length, cosy, comfortable pseudo-relationship stage that our culture specializes in. What has happened to real Christian friendship? Are we all too busy for that, or are we just so conditioned by our culture's prevailing icons that we are happier relating to a screen than to a living person? It is so much less demanding, but also so much less human.

Or what about the way 'Evangelical' churches relate to newcomers? We are great lovers of programmes, which, while not wrong in themselves, can so easily tip over into a mechanistic approach in which the individual becomes an item rather than a person. Small groups with a clearly focused syllabus can be of great benefit, provided they are a place to find meaningful relationships, and not a substitute for them. It is a truism to say that in every generation and context the church is far more conditioned and squeezed into its mould by the prevailing culture than its members either recognize or care to admit. So, in an age of number crunching, where people are processed as data items, it will be tempting for churches (especially growing ones) to follow the same pattern. Courses taught, numbers attending, information conveyed – all these are measurable and therefore attractive markers. But the sharing of deep personal burdens, the weeping with those who weep, the heart of love and concern for the needs and concerns of others – all of these can be swept aside by the aims of processed efficiency. It is not insignificant that many of the most appreciated programmes in church growth terms currently have a meal together and time to relax and get to know one another as a central ingredient to their schedule. It is only human, after all.

Within the same context, I would want also to plead for a rethink about the role and content of preaching. Over the past twenty years or so, preaching has had a bad press. We are told that it is an ineffective means of communication in a generation where attention spans are so short and that soundbite, PowerPoint presentations are a much more successful contemporary communication style. That may well be so in business or professional life, but preaching has never been primarily about conveying information. A lecture may be 'the process by which information is transferred from the lecturer's notes to the student's notes without passing through the mind of either party', but real preaching is never like that. Rather it is the work of God's Spirit by which His Word is conveyed through the mind to the heart in order to activate the will. Real preaching addresses the whole person as a person, engaging both the intellect and the emotions. It speaks from the heart of God through the heart of the preacher to the hearts of the hearers, and yet it addresses each as an individual, however large or small the congregation. Real preaching expounds the mind and will of God; it reasons and convinces, persuades and constrains the hearer to respond in a godly way; it assures and strengthens, rebukes and unsettles, comforts and stabilizes. It is the most human of activities and one of the most underestimated of our resources in building bridges into the lives of others over which the Lord Jesus can come into their lives. Far from young people being resistant to preaching that is both biblical and relevant, they greatly enjoy it and profit from it at a variety of levels within their personalities. The preacher who humbly conveys what he has taken time and trouble to hear from God through His word will communicate with great humanity and equivalent effectiveness.

Another area of great potential significance, either for the strengthening or weakening of the cause of the gospel, is the whole matter of our individuality and self-image. In an increasingly fragmented society where the experience of a loving childhood in a stable family situation is becoming much more rare; where marriage breakup and 'serial monogamy' are routine; where more and more people live alone and where job security is a thing of the past; and where isolationism, with all its attendant insecurities, is becoming endemic, depression, in its many different guises, is the way in which such stresses often push to the surface and demand to be recognized and remedied. Low self-esteem and a negative self-image are very widespread, even among outwardly confident and successful people. The culture has its own therapies in self-assertion and self-worth programmes that seek to reverse the symptoms by force of the will. But what about the Christian response? Sadly, it has often been one of denial. Too many Christians are still persuaded to sing 'Now I am happy all the day', which is clearly an impossibility in a fallen world. They are exhorted to overcome their depression by spiritual mind games or power programmes. Sometimes the alternative has been to see oneself as a helpless victim of hostile circumstances orchestrated by the devil, and to degenerate into wallowing in self-pity and paralysis.

The biblical view of personhood is more realistic and therefore more curative. It acknowledges the complexity of our humanity and the myriad ways in which we sin, are sinned against, and then sin in response to other people's sin. Analysis of causes can be helpful, but is not in itself a remedy, as every counsellor knows. True self-worth is to be found only in a right relationship with God, through the gospel. It begins when we see ourselves as God sees us – sinful, wilful, arrogant and rebellious – and are brought to face up to the depth of our guilt and culpability. This means that we shall never find the self-value we seek by looking within ourselves, but only in our relationship with Christ, for the glory of the gospel is that 'while we were still sinners, Christ died for us' (Romans 5:8). If, when we were lost and helpless, we mattered so much to God that He was prepared to send His Son to that agonizing death on the cross so that we can be justly forgiven and reconciled to Him, then there is no limit to our value in the eyes of our Redeemer. And His are the only eyes that matter, for He is both Judge and Rescuer. Our self-image becomes then that of the sinner saved by grace. In our total dependence on God and His mercy we are liberated from our dependence on ourselves or other people's views of us. We are the much-loved children of our heavenly Father, adopted into His family as heirs of His eternal inheritance. But we also realize that we are people in transition. I like the T-shirt that reads 'Be patient! God hasn't finished with me yet!' We are human beings who are Christian 'becomers', growing up into Christ.

As such, we are not surprised that life in the present continues to be a battle against the world, the flesh and the devil. Every day finds us at the cross, in renewed repentance and fresh dependence on God's gracious forgiveness. And every day finds us at the throne of heavenly grace, asking for help in our time of need and the fullness of the Spirit's power, enabling us to keep running the race and fighting the good fight. We are not immune from the ordinary pressures of life in a fallen world – sickness and pain, sorrow and disappointment, sin and failure – nor do we expect to be airlifted out of them. But we do have someone to be with us who could not love us more than He does and will never love us less. We do have a refuge in times of trial and a present help who has promised never to leave or forsake us. As fallible human beings, in all our physical, moral and spiritual fragility, we could not be more highly valued than that. It is God's commitment to our humanness that will see us home to heaven where 'there will be no more death or mourning or crying or pain, for the old order of things has passed away' (Revelation 20:4).

Such a realistic and biblical view integrates the sacred and the secular into one integrated humanity in personhood created by and being restored by the living God. There are many other areas of life that would require specialist chapters to cover adequately the implications of these foundation principles. In such areas, Bible-believing gospel people should be taking the lead. There is so much to offer our fractured culture in building strong marriages, developing loving, secure families, dealing with our sexuality and questioning our cultural presuppositions. The gospel is not just about heaven. It is about us, and it impacts our lives at every level. Far from being a religious 'add-on', it is the only metanarrative that can make sense of our humanity, set contextually in time and eternity, and provide not just a system of values but the radical dynamism to transform progressively our brokenness into the likeness of the Man from heaven. Only the gospel can actually 'put Humpty together again'. When Christians begin to demonstrate that reality in action, as well as word, the hungry world will see the ashes it feeds on for what they really are, and rejoice that the invitation to this heavenly banquet is still open.

The power of the gospel of Christ to transform a human life has rarely been seen more dramatically than in the life of John Newton (1725–1807), a profligate slave trader converted during a storm at sea and later, for over forty years, a preacher of the gospel he once despised and scorned. It is said that one of Newton's favourite sayings, doubtless reflecting his experience of God's 'amazing grace' (one of the hymns he wrote), ran like this: 'I'm not what I ought to be; but I'm not what I once was. And it is by the grace of God that I am what I am.'

That is authentic evangelical experience – humanity restored by the gospel.

* * *

Revd David Jackman is the Director of the Proclamation Trust and the Cornhill Training Course. He was formerly minister at Above Bar Church, Southampton.

5

Evangelicals and Gender

Kristin Aune

Introduction

The term 'gender', let alone the concept, is often misunder-stood by Christians. This is a fact I am familiar with. When explaining to Christians that my doctoral research is on gender in contemporary British Evangelicalism, most hear the word 'gender' as 'women'. 'Oh, so you're looking at the role of women in the church,' they say, so I explain that gender is just as much an issue of masculinity as of femininity, and that my research is concerned with more than simply female or male 'roles' in church. So, to give a necessary clarification, 'gender' in this chapter refers to *the state of being male or female* (which is produced by complex interaction between biological and social influences). It is also necessary to define two terms used for positions taken by 'Evangelicals' in the gender debate, since these will be referred to in this chapter. One is what I will term the 'male headship' position, which believes that overall church leadership, and sometimes also preaching to mixed congregations, should be carried out only by men. It sees male headship, by which it means male authority or leadership, as governing other relationships between men and women, most notably marriage. This position has variously been called 'complementarianism', 'hierarchism' and 'traditionalism'. The other is what I will call the 'egalitarian' position, which sees gift and character, rather than gender, as appropriate gauges for deciding who takes on positions of service within the church. It stresses the need for women and men's mutual submission within all their relationships, including marriage and the church. This viewpoint has also been called 'biblical feminism'.

The Twin Dangers

Distortionism

The twin dangers of distortionism and reductionism are starkly applicable to the issue of gender. Christians guilty of distortion in their understanding of gender have capitulated to pressures from society and replaced the authority of Scripture with the authority of cultural norms. This is a charge that Christians who advocate male headship level at egalitarians. They believe that egalitarians have given way to the second-wave feminist movement, reading the Bible through the eyes of an ideology that is incompatible with Christianity.[1] Yet on the whole this is an unfair charge, as virtually all egalitarian scholars have come to their position through biblical study, rather than through involvement with second-wave feminism. However, this charge *is* often true of two other groups: those termed 'feminist theologians' and those who espouse liberal Christianity.

One particular emphasis of feminist theologians should be highlighted, and this is their emphasis on *women's experience* as a criterion for biblical interpretation. To be sure, Rosemary Radford Ruether has a point when she says that theological reflection can never be objective: 'What have been called the objective sources of theology, Scripture and Tradition, are themselves codified collective human experience.' She goes on to note that historically theology has been 'based on *male* experience rather than on universal human experience' since it has been men who have authored, interpreted and preached from the biblical texts. Feminist theology is, she argues, vital in order to redress this historical imbalance and silencing of women: 'The uniqueness of feminist theology lies not in its use of the criterion of experience but rather in its use of *women's* experience, which has been almost entirely shut out of theological reflection in the past.'[2] Elisabeth Schüssler Fiorenza also advocates this new 'hermeneutical centre' of women's experience:

> The locus òr place of divine revelation and grace is therefore not the Bible or the tradition of a patriarchal church but the *ekklesia* of women and the lives of women who live the 'option for our women selves'. It is not simply 'the experience' of women but the experience of women (and all those oppressed) struggling for liberation from patriarchal oppression.[3]

But the privileging of women's experience (as a concept in itself problematic, for women and their experiences are diverse) within feminist theology ultimately moves the locus of authority from God's revelation in Christ and the biblical texts to the 'experience' of the feminist interpreter. In this it is distortionist and profoundly un-Christian.[4]

Distortionism is also present within liberal Christianity and possibly also within the postevangelical debate. Some of these Christians argue for equality of opportunity in church leadership on the basis of 'common sense', rationalism, societal norms or equal rights. Through my own doctoral research I have encountered people who justify women's leadership of churches on the grounds that 'In this day and age you can't say women can't be leaders.' While this is a line of argument that Christians may legitimately put forward after they have engaged with Scripture and asked hard questions about its interpretation, it is not a legitimate position if it is argued *without* biblical reflection, and if Western cultural ideologies are held up as supremely authoritative.

Reductionism

There is also another – in some ways opposite – danger, and
this is reductionism. It is opposite in that it is in particular evidence among Christians who most vehemently reject feminist
theology and liberal Christianity, who seek to provide a
necessary corrective to the postmodern ethical relativism of
the former positions. According to their arguments – which in
many ways are laudatory – what matters is not listening to
societal views or beginning with issues today's culture is concerned with. Rather, Christians must return to verse-by-verse
biblical exposition, their considerations set by the content of
Scripture alone. Yet the regrettable result of this has been a
selective literalism, an overplaying of certain themes, such as
judgement and penal substitution, to the neglect of others, and
most significantly, to *the neglect of the role of culture in the author-
ship and correct interpretation of the Bible*.

Selective literalism cannot and does not work. It cannot work
because it is impossible to read the Bible objectively, free from
one's own cultural background and prejudices. The various biblical documents were written in different environments and for
different purposes. We read and interpret them in yet another
historical situation, and this must be acknowledged. Not
acknowledging this leaves room for unacknowledged cultural
prejudices to distort our reading of the Bible. As Derek Tidball
has written, following John Stott, using the term fundament-
alist for those I would term selective literalists, '[they] allow
their beliefs to be uncritically influenced by their culture'.[5]
Reductionism is what in the past led missionaries to persuade
their converts that to be biblical required the adoption of particular Western societal norms in morally neutral areas such as
dress and leisure activities. These missionary practices ultimately did significant harm to the gospel's reputation.

As far as gender is concerned, selective literalism today
results in Christians reading the presuppositions about men
and women's roles of their cultural backgrounds into the
Bible and then preaching these norms as if they were biblical.
It is surely no coincidence that the British non-charismatic

'Evangelicals' (if I may make such crude categorizations) most in favour of male headship often come from upper–middle and upper-class backgrounds, which, historically, have held to a Victorian 'separate spheres' view that men should go out to work and women stay at home. Significant numbers of the charismatic 'Evangelicals' who hold to male headship began their church lives in Brethren churches where women were not permitted to speak in mixed-sex meetings.

This unconscious adoption of a Victorian 'separate spheres' mentality has especially disadvantaged women. For while some women are content to fulfil domestic and childcare roles, not all are happy, or indeed able, to fulfil these roles. Many couples cannot afford to support a family on a single income; other women have gifts and skills most appropriately used in the workplace or in Christian ministry; one quarter of adult 'Evangelical' churchgoers are single women. Many women in male headship churches, particularly those with leadership and preaching gifts, have experienced hurt and rejection on discovering that the gifts they long to use to serve the church are not wanted. Instead, they are asked only to make coffee and help with administration. My own research illustrates this marginalization of single women in 'Evangelical' churches.[6] That women lack a voice in 'Evangelicalism' is exemplified by the fact that this is the only chapter in this book written by a woman.

There have been three further consequences of the reductionist attitude to gender. The first is the disunity and polarization among 'Evangelical' Christians as to the ministry of women. Because gender had not been sufficiently addressed, the 1970s and 1980s saw the egalitarian or biblical feminist movement emerge, which began as the North American Evangelical Women's Caucus and is now based around the organizations Christians for Biblical Equality in the USA and Men, Women and God in Britain. Egalitarians wrote books, lectured, and established local networks with the aim of convincing 'Evangelicals' that biblical teaching indicated that women should take their place in ministry alongside men.[7] This later prompted a backlash from supporters of male headship in the form of the formation of the Council on Biblical Manhood and Womanhood.[8]

The proportion of 'Evangelicals' who support male headship or egalitarianism (or take a middle position) today is unknown. If the Church of England may be taken as an example, it is commonly known that the motion for ordination of women succeeded in 1992 because by that time a sufficient proportion of 'Evangelical' clergy had changed from a male headship to an egalitarian viewpoint. Yet in the wake of women's ordination, the group Reform established itself in opposition to the motion. Today, significant numbers of Anglican 'Evangelicals' will not accept female vicars or allow women to preach in their own churches. In certain male headship churches, opposition to women in church government and preaching roles has almost become a test of 'Evangelical' orthodoxy; a sign that one is a 'sound' or 'keen' Christian.

The second consequence of the reductionist view of gender is that the gendered dimension of churchgoing, and its implications and possible solutions, have been ignored. Historically, women have constituted the majority of churchgoers at least since the Victorian era, and in recent times the disparity has appeared to increase. In 1979, women made up 55 per cent of the church. Ten years later, in 1989, this figure had risen to 58 per cent. The most up-to-date figures put female church membership at between 61 and 65 per cent.[9] There is a paucity of research on the church's gender imbalance, and as yet only theories have been suggested. Some hypothesize that women's increased religiosity is due to their greater responsibility as primary childrearers in teaching their children moral values. Others claim that religion is more suited to those with a feminine personality orientation, the majority of whom will be women. Another theory states that women feel more guilt than men and are more submissive, and that since religion is dependent on its adherents submitting to God for forgiveness of sin, women are more likely to convert.[10] Male children of churchgoing parents are also more likely to drop out of church. This is because girls tend to be brought up to be more conformist than boys.[11] As I have suggested elsewhere, it may be the case that women are more active in evangelizing same-sex friends than their male counterparts. Church-based evangelistic projects are more likely to be directed at women than at men, with mother and toddler clubs and women's coffee mornings common church initiatives.[12] If the church does not see the gender imbalance as a key issue needing both practical and theological response, it is likely to continue to increase.

The third and final consequence of a reductionist view is that most Christians are unable to respond to the questions those who are not Christians are asking about gender. The nature of gender identity and the meaning of personhood are key concerns for those living in the culture of postmodernity. If the church is unable to engage with the debates about such topics as the nature and origin of gender difference, empowerment, postfeminism and the crisis in masculinity, we will lose a major opportunity for evangelism. The gospel is good news for gender as much as it is for anything else, and it is able to transform men and women's relationships and gender identities.

Thinking Evangelically about Gender

So how should we think evangelically about gender? Gender (to respond to distortionism) is something the gospel addresses sufficiently and authoritatively. We do not need to turn to alternative ideologies to find wisdom and guidance as to how to live as women or men. Gender (to respond to reductionism) must be dragged from the sidelines to occupy a prominent position. For none of us should ignore the fact that we are male or female. In everything we do, think, say; in the way we relate to others and make choices; in the way we are constrained by our backgrounds and the social circumstances we find ourselves in – in all these things we act as gendered people. If we do not believe or acknowledge this it is likely that we are allowing our expression of femininity or masculinity to be influenced by those around us rather than by the gospel. Gender is not just about marriage, the church and the nuclear family. It encompasses the whole of our lives.

The New Testament shows how the good news of the gospel affected views and expressions of gender in a number of different geographical locations and cultures. In order to demonstrate how the gospel is good news for our society in relation to gender, it is important to see how it was good news for the early church. A correct method of interpretation pays attention to cultural context – our own, that of those we are communicating the gospel to, and that of the New Testament documents and the early church – yet allows the gospel to subordinate and transform these contexts. John Stott, writing about crosscultural mission, has shown how important contextualization is:

> The overriding reason why we should take other people's cultures seriously is that God has taken ours seriously. God is the supreme communicator. And his Word has come to us in an extremely particularized form. Whether spoken or written, it was addressed to particular people in particular cultures using the particular thought-forms, syntax, and vocabulary with which they were familiar. Then when God's Word actually 'became flesh,' the 'flesh' he became was that of a first-century, male, Palestinian Jew. Thus both Inspiration and Incarnation – two fundamental evangelical truths – are models of sensitive cross-cultural communication, and summon us to follow suit … The major challenge to the worldwide Christian mission today is whether we are willing to pay the cost of following in the footsteps of our incarnate Lord in order to contextualize the Gospel. Our failure of communication is a failure of contextualization.[13]

The principle used by Jesus and the authors of the New Testament was *to work within the societal structures of the time, primarily to aid evangelism, but transform them in the light of the gospel*.[14] Understanding this elucidates what was happening with regard to gender in the early church. Although it is common to refer to the culture of the New Testament as 'the

Greco-Roman world', this does not mean that only one culture or way of living existed. There were, in fact, two main cultures in the Greco-Roman world: Hellenistic and Roman. Hellenistic (or ancient Greek) culture was concentrated in the east of the Roman Empire, while Roman culture predominated in the west. These two cultures' attitudes to gender were different, and, as a result, Paul's instructions about how the gospel should transform the existing gender roles differed.

Gender in the Hellenistic churches

Hellenistic society was based around a household structure. Many people would have lived within the household, including extended family members and slaves. The household was made up of a number of sections and was semi-public. These households were also a place of work; the separation between workplace and home that exists in the West today was not present in Hellenistic cities such as Ephesus. This household was also patriarchal and hierarchical. By law, a man was the head of the household, and his headship was a role of authority. Maintaining order was of supreme importance. The head of the household would often require his whole household to serve his gods, which is why a whole household would often convert to Christianity shortly after their master had done so. Only he and a few favoured male slaves had a public role and were able to move outside the household within the city. Women lacked a public role and could not work outside the home. Marriage was not done for love, but to bear legitimate children to continue the family line. The average age for a man to marry was thirty; for a woman it was less than eighteen. This age difference added to the subordinate status of the woman, who was viewed as the property of her husband, and who had very few legal rights. A woman's failure to produce a son was often considered grounds for divorcing her. Because men saw their wives simply as childbearers, many men (and some women) were promiscuous, having mistresses and concubines. The modern idea that men and women were equal, or were companions, was entirely absent. Men and women did not eat meals together, and a woman's place was indoors, at the rear of the household.

When people in Hellenistic societies such as Ephesus accepted the gospel, they did so within this household structure. Indeed, Paul in Ephesians uses the metaphor of the household for the church: 'You are... fellow-citizens with God's people and members of God's household, built on the foundation of the apostles and prophets, with Christ Jesus himself as the chief cornerstone' (Ephesians 2:19–20).[15] One of the primary reasons why the household structure was retained, along with a small differentiation in gender roles, was for the sake of outside observers: it was an aid to evangelism. Titus 2 shows this. Older women are told to train the younger women to be busy at home and subject to their husbands 'so that no-one will malign the word of God' (v. 5). Similarly, slaves are to be taught to be subject to their masters 'so that in every way they will make the teaching about God our Saviour attractive' (v. 10). Likewise, in 1 Peter 3 the reason for the wives' submission to their non-Christian husbands is 'so that, if any of them do not believe the word, they may be won over without words' (v. 1), in other words, for the sake of evangelism. In 1 Timothy 2:15, women are instructed to return to childbearing roles for the sake of 'propriety'.

Yet though the household remained the structure within which the gospel was worked out, it was transformed. This is evident in the way that Paul uses gospel concepts to describe it. It now belonged not to the householder but to God. The central symbol of their faith, the meal of bread and wine, was a whole-church affair: no longer did men and women eat separately. Within the household, marriage, and the gender roles within it, were transformed in the light of the gospel. All Christians were to 'submit to one another out of reverence for Christ' (Ephesians 5:21). While husbands remained the head of their wives and the masters of their slaves, the meaning of headship changed. Where before love had been absent from marriage, now the husbands are told three times, in verses 25, 28 and 33, to 'love your wives'. No longer did the husband's headship entail authority over his wife – that concept is entirely absent from the instructions in Ephesians 5. Rather, headship now meant modelling the relationship of Christ with His church, giving himself up for her, feeding and caring for her as he would do his own body.

If this is the case with marriage in male headship societies, what about ministry? Paul's first letter to Timothy concerns the Hellenistic Ephesian church, and it is here that the only New Testament prohibition against women teaching or having authority over men appears. Indeed, the only two New Testament passages restricting women's roles (1 Timothy 2:11–12 and 1 Corinthians 14:34–35) were both addressed to Hellenistic churches. The Ephesians 2:19 description of the church as God's household is recalled in 1 Timothy 3:15. The purpose of the letter is the countering of false teaching, which had become rife in the Ephesian church. This is evident by the fact that Paul both begins and ends the letter with references to false teaching. He begins, 'As I urged you when I went into Macedonia, stay there in Ephesus so that you may command certain persons not to teach false doctrines any longer' (1:3), explaining that 'some have wandered away... and turned to meaningless talk' (1:6). He concludes: 'Timothy, guard what has been entrusted to your care. Turn away from godless chatter and the opposing ideas of what is falsely called knowledge, which some have professed and in so doing have wandered from the faith' (6:20–21).

What was women's role in this false teaching? Chapter 4:3 shows that the false teaching forbids marriage. That women had a key role in spreading it is evident. In chapter 4:7 it is referred to as 'old wives tales'. According to chapter 5:

> [younger widows] get into the habit of being idle and going about from house to house. And not only do they become idlers, but also gossips[16] and busybodies, saying things they ought not to. So I counsel younger widows to marry, to have children, to manage their homes and to give the enemy no opportunity for slander. Some have in fact already turned away to follow Satan. (vv. 13–15)

2 Timothy 3:6 provides corroboration that women had become influenced by false teaching; false teachers had wormed their

way into the homes of 'weak-willed women' and gained control over them. We can only speculate, but it may be the case that women were able to spread this false teaching precisely because they had experienced freedom from some of their role restrictions on becoming Christians. To summarize what was happening, in Ephesus women had become taken in by heretical teaching and were now spreading it. Many of these women were young widows who were now teaching that marriage and childbearing were bad. This teaching was so dangerous that they were in danger of losing their salvation.

It is impossible to be sure exactly what the heretical teaching consisted of, but it may well have been Gnosticism, and this would make perfect sense of the references to Adam and Eve in 2:13–14. In 6:20 Paul calls this teaching 'what is falsely called *knowledge*', using the word gnõsis. Gnostics particularly revered Eve and praised her eating from the tree because, they believed, this brought knowledge to human beings. They also believed that she was created before Adam, and claimed that women, following Eve, were mediators of special and superior revelations. In this light, it is easy to see Paul's purpose in verses 11–15:

> A woman should learn in quietness and full submission. I do not permit a woman to teach or to have authority over a man; she must be silent. For Adam was formed first, then Eve. And Adam was not the one who was deceived; it was the woman who was deceived and became a sinner. But women will be saved through childbearing – if they continue in faith, love and holiness with propriety.

Instead of teaching heresy, Paul tells women to learn. Women at that time had little or no education, which may be one reason why they were so easily influenced by false teaching. In verse 12 the tense of 'I do not permit' is the present continuous, rendering the meaning 'I am not *presently* permitting'; this is a culture-dependent prohibition. If the heresy is Gnosticism, verses 13–14 show Paul countering the Gnostic myths about women's superiority. No, Eve wasn't created *before* Adam but *after*, he says. Furthermore, Eve was the first sinner, which negates any claim that women are spiritually superior. But even if the heresy was not Gnosticism, the verses must still be read as a culture-dependent prohibition. The word translated 'authority' is not the normal New Testament word for authority. It means something like 'domineer' and points to the activity of the women spreading false teaching. Paul then recalls the Fall: just as Eve was deceived by the serpent, these women had been deceived by false teachers. This cannot be made to imply that women are inherently more deceivable than men. A claim for the reverse could just as easily be made with reference to Romans 5:12, where Paul makes a similar point but this time only attributes blame to Adam: 'Just as sin entered the world through *one man*.' The thrust of 1 Timothy 2:11–15 is that the women must do the opposite of what they had been doing. They must stop their noisy, domineering false teaching, learn true doctrine and turn back to marriage and bearing children. This would be how they would keep their salvation. This prohibition against women teaching or having authority is not for all time. Indeed, evidence from elsewhere, particularly from the Roman churches, suggests that women were teaching and leading some of the early churches.

Gender in the Roman churches

Gender roles in Roman society were much more fluid and women had considerable freedom. Women had a far greater public role and almost the same rights as men. They could own property, manage their own finances, run a business and institute divorce proceedings against their husbands. Not surprisingly, the churches in the New Testament in which women held leadership and teaching roles were situated in the Roman part of the Greco-Roman world. The churches at Philippi and Rome are examples of this. The first person to become a Christian in the Roman colony of Philippi, in Macedonia, was Lydia, a dealer in purple cloth. Her occupation marks her out as a businesswoman of particularly high status. Lydia was in charge of her own household, and her conversion was followed by the baptism of the entire household (Acts 16:12–15). The letter to the Philippians shows that in such a culture, women's church roles were greater, demonstrating that women and men worked alongside each other in the gospel. Paul describes two women, Euodia and Syntyche, as having 'contended at my side in the cause of the gospel, along with Clement and the rest of my co-workers' (Philippians 4:3). An interpretation that has these women working under Paul's authority, or in purely supportive roles, cannot be derived from the text.

Romans 16 provides the most conclusive evidence that women took leading roles in Roman churches. Paul begins his list of greetings by commending Phoebe, who, it appears, was coming to work with the church in Rome. Phoebe is described as a 'servant', 'deacon' or 'minister'; this word is translated 'deacon' in 1 Timothy 3:11. She is also a benefactor or protector, as verse 2 demonstrates. There is no mention of her needing to be accompanied on her journey by a man, or of her being married. Most scholars conclude that she was a church leader. The fact that Paul begins his greetings with Phoebe indicates that she was prominent in the church. Priscilla and Aquila, the couple who appear several times in the New Testament, are mentioned in verse 3 as Paul's 'co-workers in Christ Jesus'. Priscilla is mentioned first, as she is in the majority of references to her and her husband in the New Testament, which implies her greater significance. Paul employs the term 'co-workers' elsewhere for his chief associates in his apostolic mission, and so it cannot be read simply as denoting supportive, background gospel work. Acts 18:26 corroborates this: here Priscilla and Aquila are seen expounding the word of God to Apollos, who became an influential church leader.

Verses 6 and 12 present Mary, Tryphaena, Tryphosa and Persis, four women who 'work hard in the Lord'. Again, the verb used here is the one Paul uses of his associates' apostolic ministry. In verse 7 he greets Andronicus and Junia, who are likely to be husband and wife, and are noted apostles, meaning that they had an evangelistic and church-building ministry. Until the Middle Ages no one questioned Junia's gender, but gradually certain New Testament translators began to change the feminine Junia to Junias, a man's name, because they were unable to believe that a woman could have been an apostle. Either out of ignorance or out of a desire to remove the evidence of Junia's existence, they were willing to overlook the fact that the man's name Junias did not even exist at the time the letter to the Romans was written.

Implications for Today

The effect of the gospel on gender in the Greco-Roman world was radical, yet it was radical within the societal structures of the time. As we have seen, within the New Testament a principle is applied as regards the relation of the gospel to culture. As was done in Hellenistic and Roman churches, being evangelical requires Christians to *work within the societal structures of the time, primarily to aid evangelism, but transform them in the light of the gospel*. To relate this principle to church life today leads to four conclusions:

Women's ministry

Given that Western societies enshrine gender equality in law, ministry needs to involve women alongside men at all levels. To forbid women leadership or preaching roles would be to violate Paul's principle and to hinder evangelism. Many people reject the church not because they object to the gospel, but because of the church's record of oppressing women (and, historically, non-white people): because the gospel has been seen to be not good but bad news for women. This immediately creates a barrier that prevents them from listening to any presentation of the gospel that Christians might give.

Inclusive language for humans

Western society also considers the implications of the language it uses. The media follow a code that seeks to avoid unnecessary sexism, recognizing, for example, that the use of the word 'men' to mean 'people' excludes women and obscures the true meaning of the term. Where 'men' used to be understood as meaning 'people', now Westerners are highly attuned to instances in which language is ambiguous or women's existence is ignored. To many, not to use inclusive language is an affront to women's humanity. The church needs to be sensitive to this, and, where possible, use language and Bible translations that account for the recent shift in linguistic use. Translations such as the New International Version Inclusive Language Edition and the New Revised Standard Version follow this principle, using inclusive terminology such as 'people' rather than 'men', 'brothers and sisters' rather than 'brothers', and 'sons and daughters' rather than 'sons' where the original Hebrew and Greek carry the more inclusive meaning. In this, they provide a clearer, more accurate translation.

Marriage

The fact that Paul compares male headship to the relationship between Christ and the church in Ephesians 5 does not mean that male headship itself is an eternal concept, as some would argue. To believe this would require that slavery also be upheld as an eternal concept, for Paul uses eternal gospel truths to describe the relationship between slaves and their masters, telling them to submit to their masters as they would to Christ (Ephesians 6:5–7; Colossians 3:22–24). To claim that male headship is eternal is to misunderstand the use of metaphor and to miss Paul's crucial principle. Rather, gospel truths (such as the relationship between Christ and the church) enable Christians to transform the different environments in which they find themselves – whether these environments are male headship societies, difficult work situations or egalitarian marriages. Servant headship is not necessarily a bad model for Christian marriages in the West today, yet it is likely to be inadvisable to attempt to use a model based on a past societal structure in which we do not and cannot live today. Rather, it is our task to transform the modern notion of marriage through the gospel.

In Western society divorce rates are high, and so Christian marriage will require lifelong fidelity, mirroring God's faithfulness to us. In Western society marriage is undertaken for romantic love; Christian marriage will involve love that is also sacrificial, symbolizing Christ's sacrifice for us. Western marriage can be selfish; Christian marriage should involve mutual submission, mirroring the relationships within the Trinity.

Engaging with society

Gender is an enduring fascination within contemporary society and provides Christians with a significant opportunity for dialogue and transformation. When Christians eschew distortionism and reductionism they will find themselves liberated to explore and express the gospel's transforming power over contemporary concepts of masculinity and femininity. How could the gospel transform today's women's dilemmas over work and motherhood within a culture that considers child-rearing the prime responsibility of the mother, yet creates economic conditions which require her, whether or not she chooses to do so, to engage in paid employment? How could the gospel transform the lives of today's young women, who look forward to greater respect in the workplace, yet at the same time live within a highly sexualized culture in which their physical attractiveness is considered more important than ever? How could the gospel address challenge manifestations both of male crisis and male dominance? An evangelical response to these issues must not simply be theoretical; it must also be practically incarnated in the whole lives of churches, friends, families and individuals. As Germaine Greer so aptly challenged some three decades ago, what will you do?

* * *

Kristin Aune is completing a PhD thesis on gender in contemporary British evangelicalism at King's College, London. She is the author of *Single Women: Challenge to the Church?*

(Carlisle: Paternoster, 2002). She is Visiting Lecturer in Sociology and Women's Studies at the University of Westminster.

Notes

1 Mary Kassian takes this perspective, arguing that 'Biblical feminists seek to retain an evangelical base while at the same time modifying Biblical interpretation to be sympathetic to the concerns of the women's movement. However, in order to embrace both, Biblical feminists need to compromise the Bible.' Mary A. Kassian, *The Feminist Gospel: The Movement to Unite Feminism with the Church* (Wheaton, Illinois: Crossway, 1992), p. 217.

2 Rosemary Radford Ruether, *Sexism and God-Talk: Towards a Feminist Theology* (London: SCM Press, 1983), pp. 12–13

3 Elisabeth Schüssler Fiorenza 'The Will to Choose or Reject: Continuing our Critical Work' in Letty Russell (ed.), *Feminist Interpretation of the Bible* (Oxford: Basil Blackwell, 1985), p. 128.

4 For a helpful theological critique of feminist theology, see Linda Woodhead, 'Spiritualising the Sacred: A Critique of Feminist Theology' in *Modern Theology* vol.13, no.2, April 1997, pp. 191–212.

5 Derek J. Tidball, *Who Are the Evangelicals?: Tracing the Roots of the Modern Movements* (London: Marshall Pickering, 1991), p. 17, based on John Stott in David L. Edwards and John Stott, *Essentials: A Liberal–Evangelical Dialogue* (London: Hodder & Stoughton, 1988), p. 91.

6 Kristin Aune, *Single Women: Challenge to the Church?* (Carlisle: Paternoster, 2002).

7 The web site for Christians for Biblical Equality is www.cbeinter national.org. Men, Women and God can be contacted at men womenandgod@yahoo.co.uk. Significant publications arguing this perspective are: Mary J. Evans, *Woman in the Bible* (Carlisle: Paternoster, 1983); Gilbert Bilezikian, *Beyond Sex Roles* (Grand Rapids: Baker, 1985); Gretchen Gaebelein Hull, *Equal to Serve: Women and Men in the Church and Home* (London: Scripture Union, 1989); Martin Scott, *The Role and Ministry of Women* (Milton

Keynes: Word, 1992); and the forthcoming Ronald W. Pierce, Rebecca Merrill Groothuis and Gordon D. Fee (eds), *Discovering Biblical Equality: Complementarity Without Hierarchy* (Grand Rapids, Michigan: Baker, 2003).

8 The web site for the Council on Biblical Manhood and Womanhood is www.cbmw.org. Its British web site is www.cbmw.org.uk. Significant publications arguing this perspective are: James Hurley, *Man and Woman in Biblical Perspective: A Study in Role Relationships and Authority* (Leicester: Inter-Varsity Press, 1981); Susan T. Foh, *Women and the Word of God: A Response to Biblical Feminism* (Grand Rapids: Baker, 1981); J. David Pawson, Leadership is Male: A Challenge to Christian Feminism (Crowborough: Highland, 1988); and John Piper and Wayne Grudem (eds), *Recovering Biblical Manhood and Womanhood: A Response to Evangelical Feminism* (Wheaton, Illinois: Crossway, 1991).

9 The figure of 61 per cent is quoted in Heather Wraight, *Eve's Glue: The Role Women Play in Holding the Church Together* (Carlisle: Paternoster, 2001), p. 21. The figure of 65 per cent is quoted in Churches Information for Mission, *Faith in Life: A Snapshot of Church Life at the Beginning of the 21st Century* (London: Churches Information for Mission, 2001), p. 9.

10 For an overview of theories of religious differences between men and women, see William K. Kay and Leslie J. Francis, *Drift from the Churches: Attitude toward Christianity During Childhood and Adolescence* (Cardiff: University of Wales Press, 1996), pp. 10–16.

11 Hart M. Nelsen, 'Religious Conformity in an Age of Disbelief: Contextual Effects of Time, Denomination, and Family Processes upon Church Decline and Apostasy', *American Sociological Review* 46 (1981), pp. 632–40.

12 Aune, *Single Women*, p. 18.

13 John Stott, 'Foreword' in John R.W. Stott and Robert Coote (eds), *Down to Earth: Studies in Christianity and Culture – The Papers of the Lausanne Consultation on Gospel and Culture* (London: Hodder & Stoughton, 1981), pp. vii–viii.

14 I am particularly grateful for Gordon Fee and R.T. France's work on this. See Gordon Fee's 'Gender Issues: Reflections on the Perspective of the Apostle Paul' in Gordon D. Fee, *Listening to the*

Spirit in the Text (Grand Rapids: Eerdmans, 2000) and 'The Cultural Context of Ephesians 5:18–6:9, *Priscilla Papers*, vol.16, no.1, Winter 2002, pp. 3–8. R.T. France's work includes *Women in the Church's Ministry: A Test-Case for Biblical Hermeneutics* (Carlisle: Paternoster, 1995) and *A Slippery Slope?: The Ordination of Women and Homosexual Practice – A Case Study in Biblical Interpretation* (Cambridge: Grove, 2000). I have also been helped by James R. Payton's 'A Tale of Two Cultures', *Priscilla Papers* vol.16, no.1, Winter 2002, pp. 13–17. *Priscilla Papers* is the journal of Christians for Biblical Equality.

15 All quotations are taken from *The Holy Bible, New International Version, Inclusive Language Edition: The New Testament, Psalms and Proverbs* (London: Hodder & Stoughton, 1995).

16 The NIV translation 'gossips' is misleading, as this would imply idle talk about other people's lives. Rather, says Gordon Fee, the Greek word 'means to talk nonsense, or foolishness, and is used most often in contexts of speaking something foolish or absurd in comparison to the truth. Thus, the young widows are described in terms very much like the false teachers.' See Gordon D. Fee, *New International Biblical Commentary: 1 and 2 Timothy, Titus* (Carlisle: Paternoster, 1995), p. 122.

6

Evangelicals and the Bible

Paul Blackham

Much could be written on a properly evangelical understanding of the nature and use of Scripture. Much too could be said about how parts of the 'Evangelical' constituency fail to treat God's written word in a thoroughly evangelical way. Here, however, we shall treat only one element of a truly evangelical understanding of Scripture – but this is nevertheless a crucial part of what it means to be biblical and should not, therefore, be ignored or misunderstood.

This crucial element is the doctrine of the sufficiency of Scripture, or what the Reformers maintained by the maxim *sola scriptura*. The principle of *sola scriptura* is one of the most continuously controversial parts of Reformation theology, and it remains controversial for large sections of an Evangelicalism that often undermines it in practice. Indeed, the radical nature of the sufficiency of Scripture is most severely controversial the more one understands the principle.

In many theological textbooks it is presented in its very weakest form – that is, as a *material* principle, that Scripture is the only source of our knowledge of the revelation of the living God. To state the principle in that way is radical enough – it cuts through the baggage of so much theological method – but it is only half the story. The principle of *sola scriptura* is only thoroughly grasped when it is presented in its true form – that Scripture is the sole authority in both a material and a formal sense. Scripture is not just the sole source of our knowledge of the revelation of God. Scripture is also the sole rule for the interpretation of Scripture.

Before we get into this, it is worth clarifying that the claim is not that God has revealed Himself *only* in the text of the canonical books of Scripture, but that any and every revelation of God is known only from the perspective of His revelation in and through the text of the Bible. This is not a detraction from the fact that all knowledge of God is Christological, in that Christ is the content of Scripture. Scripture is not the *supreme* authority, as if it could be supplemented by any other authority. Rather, the only authority that the church, reason, experience or tradition has is what Scripture itself gives to them. There is no theological authority either alongside or even supportive of the sole authority of the Bible. This will become clear as I set out the thinking of Martin Luther and John Calvin.

I propose that we investigate the great Reformers under three headings:

- What is the purpose of Scripture?
- How is Scripture authenticated?
- How is Scripture interpreted?

Martin Luther

What is the purpose of Scripture?

Luther takes note of the different styles of literature within the Bible, yet he constantly claims that Scripture has but one content – Jesus Christ. 'There is no doubt that all the Scripture points to Christ alone.'[1] 'All of Scripture everywhere deals only with Christ.'[2] Luther sees the whole of the Bible under the headings of law and gospel, but both law and gospel find their logic only in Christ. The sole purpose of law and gospel is to present Jesus Christ. In this way Luther notes that Moses had only one interest in life – leading the people of Israel to faith in Christ. When we recognize this purpose in the Old Testament, just as much as the New, then we have grasped the true purpose of the Scriptures.

How is Scripture authenticated?

Luther argues vigorously against the Roman Catholic claim that Scripture is guaranteed by the church. If this were so then the church would stand above Scripture. Luther uses the analogy of John the Baptist – John the Baptist does not guarantee or authorize or validate Jesus Christ simply by pointing at Him. In fact, it is John the Baptist who is validated as a true prophet because he correctly identifies Jesus Christ. The Scriptures are self-authenticating and in this way the church is given authority, in that the church is authorized to bear witness to Jesus Christ according to the Scriptures.

So, if the Scriptures cannot be validated by any external authority, then how exactly are they self-authenticating? The Holy Spirit causes the Scriptures to be heard as the very word of God in the ears of sinful humanity. Luther makes no distinction between the Bible authenticating itself and the Spirit authenticating Scripture. These two ideas are synonymous in his thought.

How is Scripture interpreted?

Luther carries the point of authentication into interpretation. If an outside authority is able to determine the true meaning of the Bible then that authority stands over the Bible. 'Scripture is therefore its own light. It is a grand thing when scripture interprets itself.'[3]

He observes that the mind of the author can only be grasped in what they have actually written. Any attempt to access the mind of the author in some other way – such as from historical reconstruction – is unfruitful. This has great significance for his handling of the Old Testament. Moses is an apostle of Jesus Christ – the gospel preached by Moses is exactly the same gospel preached by the New Testament apostles. The only point of difference is that Moses looked forward whereas the apostles looked back. The gospel has always been a matter of justification by faith alone in Christ alone since the beginning of the world. Luther has no time for ideas of progressive revelation. Luther speaks of the Old Testament believers as the church of Jesus Christ:

> The patriarchs had the same faith and also the same Christ. He was just as close to them as he is to us, as Hebrews 13 says, 'Jesus Christ the same yesterday, today and forever,' that is, Christ is present from the beginning of the world until its end and all are preserved through him and in him.[4]

Thus Luther does not try to confine the theological truths of the earlier books to a hypothetical embryonic faith, allowing it to slowly grow as the history of the world develops, in the manner of the theory of progressive revelation. Rather, the whole gospel of Jesus Christ is set out from the very first page of the Bible. 'Times change, as to things, bodies, tribulations, but the same Spirit, the same meaning, the same food and drink abide in all and through all.'[5] So Scripture interprets itself in presenting to us the same message at all times and in all places. There is no other vantage point from which to understand the Bible – no external theory of history or philosophy, no external research or ecclesiastical teaching can determine the true meaning of the Bible.

Luther uses this insight against both Rome and the radical Anabaptists. As Paul Althaus points out:

> each of these opponents claimed that something else than Scripture itself validates the interpretation of Scripture. In Rome, it was the teaching office of the church to which the Holy Spirit had been promised. Among the enthusiasts, it was

the peculiar gift of the Spirit who is given to individuals apart from the scripture. Luther also knows that only men who are moved by the Spirit of God can interpret the scripture. But the Spirit which enables them to interpret scripture comes to them through the scripture itself... Luther clearly recognised that Rome and the enthusiasts were in this respect both 'enthusiasts'. They both subjected the scripture to an alien law.[6]

So it is by studying the entire content of the Bible that we come to understand what it has to say in any part. The parts must be related to each other, and in this way the Scriptures govern their own meaning. But this inevitably means that the Scriptures are perspicuous. Luther notes that the Roman position is based on the idea that the Bible is an obscure book. He speaks of it as simple and clear. He gathers together a variety of biblical verses to show this. Thus perspicuity is not Luther's theological inference but part of the teaching of Scripture itself. It is a light shining in a dark place (2 Peter 1:19).

So why is there such controversy over the interpretation of the Bible? Luther does not blame the Bible for this – it is rather the influence of the world, the flesh and the devil. He explains that 'the godless are held captive by Satan and God allows even godly men to err for a while so that he may in this way show them that he alone is able to enlighten them'.[7] Left to ourselves in our sinful impotence, Luther comments that we could not see 'one single iota in scripture' – meaning that, although Scripture has an objective simplicity and clarity, it is subjectively seen as incomprehensible to the godless mind.

So, 'in itself' Scripture may be easily understood by comparing each part of Scripture with the rest of Scripture, but this clarity may only be appreciated by the illumination of the Holy Spirit. Thus the very simplest of all believers is able to comprehend Scripture better than the most sophisticated and learned unbelieving scholar.

John Calvin

What is the purpose of the Scriptures?

Calvin agrees that the purpose of Scripture is the presentation of Jesus Christ, but he develops this into a wider account, co-ordinating all of God's revelatory work under the rule of Scripture. Calvin notes that even the most excellent and sincere god language formulated outside the Bible is nothing but 'the ravings or evil imaginings of our flesh, and corrupt by our vanity the pure truth of God'.[8] All natural theology is wicked idolatry, not because God's revelation of Himself through creation is misleading, but 'such is our stupidity that we grow increasingly dull toward so manifest testimonies, and they flow away without profiting us'.[9]

Scripture is God's remedy for this hopeless situation.

> Just as old or bleary-eyed men and those with weak vision, if you thrust before them a most beautiful volume, even if they recognise it to be some sort of writing, yet can scarcely construe two words, but with the aid of spectacles will begin to read distinctly; so scripture, gathering up the otherwise confused knowledge of God in our minds, having dispersed our dullness, clearly shows us the true God.[10]

The purpose of Scripture then is not just a presentation of Christ in the gospel, but also the framework by which we are able to understand the whole of creation.

> Suppose we ponder how slippery is the fall of the human mind into forgetfulness of God, how great the tendency to every kind of error, how great the lust to fashion constantly new and artificial religions. Then we may perceive how necessary was such written proof of the heavenly doctrine, that it should neither perish through forgetfulness nor vanish through error nor be corrupted by the audacity of men... We must come, I say, to the Word, where God is truly and vividly described to us from his

works, while these very works are appraised not by our depraved judgement but by the rule of eternal truth.[11]

So Scripture both instructs the elect in the knowledge of God in Jesus Christ and also opens our eyes to the revelation of God in His works throughout the creation. All knowledge of God is inaccessible other than through the lens of Scripture. Scripture alone guides us into the knowledge of God the Creator and Redeemer. 'Christ was always exhibited to the holy fathers under the law as the object toward which they should direct their faith.'[12] Calvin goes on to say that the fathers, when they wished to behold God, always turned their eyes to Christ.

How is Scripture authenticated?

Calvin's initial concern when he turns to the authority of the Bible is to show that this authority is in no way founded upon the church. The Bible can only have its true authority when it is recognized to be the very word of God. Yet the Roman theologians ask: 'How can anyone know that this book is the word of God unless the church validates it as such?' Calvin replies:

> They mock the Holy Spirit when they ask: Who can convince us that these writings came from God? Who can assure us that scripture has come down whole and intact even to our very day? Who can persuade us to receive one book in reverence but to exclude another, unless the church prescribe a sure rule for all these matters? ...it is as if someone asked: Whence will we learn to distinguish light from darkness, white from black, sweet from bitter? Indeed, scripture exhibits fully as clear evidence of its own truth as white and black things do of their colour, or sweet and bitter things do of their taste.[13]

But surely the two things are not the same? The character of black and white is not disputed so much as the character of the Bible. Although Scripture is the sole authority in the knowledge of God, it is not less opposed than God's revelation in the creation. If we wish to apprehend Scripture as the very word of God, 'we ought to seek our conviction in a higher place than human reasons, judgements, or conjectures – that is, in the inner testimony of the Spirit'.[14]

Although Calvin confesses that the Bible is free from all errors and contradictions in the original autographs he does not build the authority of the Bible on the inerrancy of the text. To do this would be to force us into a defence of the authority of the Bible. Inerrancy for Calvin is not a demonstrable truth, but the assumption given by the witness of the Spirit.

> Let this point therefore stand: that those whom the Holy Spirit has inwardly taught truly rest upon scripture, and that scripture indeed is self-authenticated... hence it is not right to subject it to proof and reasoning... For even if it wins reverence for itself by its own majesty, it seriously affects us only when it is sealed upon our hearts through the Spirit... We seek no proofs, no marks of genuineness upon which our judgement may lean; but we subject our judgement and wit to it as to a thing far beyond any guesswork![15]

In this way Calvin rejects all apologetics. Scripture cannot be rendered authoritative or reasonable to the unbelieving mind by any amount of clever human argument. Rather, only the believer recognizes the character of Scripture because only the believer experiences the seal of the Spirit. The genuine witness of the Spirit is differentiated from the witness of all evil spirits because the witness of the Spirit corresponds exactly to the teaching of the Bible. We recognize the Spirit from the word and the word from the Spirit.

How is Scripture interpreted?

If Scripture is only recognized for what it is by the work of the Spirit, this is certainly no less true of the interpretation of the Bible. Although Calvin also (with Luther) is careful to reject all fanciful methods, those that do not rest on the plain grammatical meaning of the words, yet even the most careful methods will not provide a true understanding of the teaching of the Bible without the illumination of the Spirit. Christ is presented to us throughout Scripture, but 'nothing is accomplished by preaching him if the Spirit, as our inner teacher, does not show our minds the way... The man who depends upon the light of nature, he, I say, comprehends nothing of God's spiritual mysteries.'[16]

But was not the purpose of the Bible to correct our vision? Surely the simple words of the Bible are easily understood by anybody and from this simple exercise in 'English comprehension' a clear understanding of truth is attained.

> Let no Pelagian babble here that God remedies this stupidity or, if you will, ignorance, when he directs man's understanding by the teaching of the Word to that which it could not have reached without guidance... God's Word shines upon men; but they do not have its benefit until he who is called the 'Father of lights' [James 1:17] either gives eyes or opens them. For wherever the Spirit does not cast his light, all is darkness... He who attributes any more understanding to himself is all the more blind because he does not recognize his own blindness.[17]

Calvin doesn't want to suggest that the true meaning of the Scripture is found in esoteric allegories or subtle schemes. He states that 'the true meaning of scripture is what is plain and simple'.[18] This does not mean that each individual can make of the words of Scripture what they wish, for Calvin also holds to the perspicuity of Scripture. The believing community, by the illumination of the Spirit, is enabled to understand the plain and simple meaning of the Bible. Whereas our contemporary obsessions tend to be about hermeneutical procedures, Luther and Calvin spend far more time on the really fundamental matter of the illumination of the Holy Spirit.

The basic conviction as to the method of interpreting Scripture is that Scripture itself teaches us how to handle the Bible. The Bible contains numerous examples of biblical exegesis, and these are to form our manual of hermeneutics.

Lessons for Today

So, having reminded ourselves of the Reformers' understanding of the doctrine of the sole authority of Scripture, we should relate this to our contemporary situation. Edward Dowey points out that whereas the threat to *sola scriptura* came from the Anabaptists and the Roman Catholics in the sixteenth century, today it comes from the critical methods that wish to find the truth in the history that lies beneath the text.[19] Klaus Scholder's book *The Birth of Modern Critical Theology*[20] shows that the origins of biblical criticism lie in the advent of rationalism in the seventeenth century. A fundamental shift was being advocated. If the real master of truth was science and philosophy, then theology had to retire from the public square. Increasingly it was argued that theology could deal only with eternal, *interior* truths, whereas the *exterior* world of 'fact' and history belonged to reason.

This is where historical–critical methods began. The Bible is utterly founded on history – if the realm of history is not an area about which the Bible may speak with authority, then the Bible must wait upon the critical sciences to determine what it can or cannot say. Theology is at best a handmaid to historical criticism.

What was different was that the new judge of Scripture was not Scripture but autonomous reason. The greatest advocates of historical–critical methods were not enemies of the Bible, but were those who wanted to argue *for* orthodox Christian theology on a new foundation. The first generation of the critical theologians arrived at the same conclusions as their evangelical forefathers, but their conclusions had a very different authority.

Once science and philosophy are acknowledged to rule the worlds of 'fact' and history then the Bible may never speak in its own words. Karl Barth in his *Church Dogmatics* begins with a careful exposition of this truth.

> When our alleged faith is brought face to face with this fact, it
> is seen to repose only upon the cunning conclusion that God

has made out His case in accordance with *our* well-founded convictions. Even the most positive result of this process, perhaps squaring exactly in vocabulary with the bible and with every traditional dogma, will make no difference to the fact that it is certainly not God's revelation that we have recognised in this way... It should be noted that theological neo-Protestantism in its beginnings... could deal with bible and dogma in a thoroughly conservative way. Nevertheless, even in these conservative forms it means misconstruction, nay, denial of revelation.[21]

When the fathers of historical criticism, Hermann Samuel Reimarus and Gotthold Lessing, treated the Bible 'like any other book' they were doing nothing more than consistently expressing the new structure of authority.[22] Lessing was the most self-aware about what he was doing. He writes: 'Religion is not true because the evangelists and apostles taught it; but they taught it because it is true. The written traditions must be interpreted by their inward truth and no written traditions can give the religion any inward truth if it has none.'[23]

In *On the Proof of the Spirit and of Power* Lessing takes it for granted that the world of the Bible is not the world of the eighteenth century. The title of the book is taken from Origen's statement that the truth of the Bible is demonstrated in the Spirit and in power – a Spirit and power that were not only at work in the world of the Bible but continued to be at work in Origen's world. Lessing writes:

I am no longer in Origen's position; I live in the eighteenth century, in which miracles no longer happen... The problem is that this proof of the spirit and of power no longer has any spirit or power, but has sunk to the level of human testimonies of spirit and power.[24]

Of course, it is hard for us to suppress a snigger at Lessing's expense. The eighteenth century was marked by some of the most amazing manifestations of the Spirit and of power in the evangelical awakenings in Britain and America. While

Lessing was wringing his hands over the powerlessness of the Bible, John Wesley was writing accounts of the utter power-fulness of the gospel in his journals.

This brings us closer to our goal. For Lessing, the Bible is a book of historical testimony that must be judged alongside other testimonies. For Wesley, the Bible is not about what was once said, but it is the venue where God *continues* to speak in Spirit and in power.

Historical–critical methods approach the Bible as a testimony to be assessed and dissected, and it is this that can no longer be sustained in our own day. Today, who has any confidence in the objectivity that seemed so glamorous in the eighteenth century?

It is fascinating to read Karl Barth's letters and papers from the early 1920s. His liberal teachers had been deeply committed to establishing biblical studies on the foundation of histori-cal–critical methods, engaging in what they called scientific theology. Yet Barth could see that to do such a thing was to establish one's real authority outside the text of the Bible. In the Barth–Harnack correspondence of 1923 the collision between the two approaches could hardly be clearer.[25]

Harnack puts fifteen questions to his former pupil, entitled 'Fifteen Questions to the Despisers of Scientific Theology'. The questions are very frank and specific. For example:

> 2. Is the religion of the Bible, or are its revelations, so com-pletely a unity and so clear that historical knowledge and critical reflection are not needed for a correct understanding of their meaning?

> 14. If the person of Jesus Christ stands at the centre of the gospel, how else can the basis for reliable and communal knowledge of this person be gained but through critical–historical study...? What besides scientific theology is able to undertake this study?

> 15. ...is there any other theology than that which has strong ties, and is in blood-relationship with science in general? Should there be one, what persuasiveness and value belong to it?[26]

Harnack was asking how the interpretation of the Bible could be saved from the subjective opinions of individual Christians. How could we know what Jesus was really like apart from through critical–historical research? And how can theology ignore the findings of science? Barth's answers to these questions are incisive.

2. ...[the Bible] is understood through neither this or that 'function of the soul or mind' but by virtue of *that* Spirit which is identical with the content of the bible, and that by *faith*.

14. The reliability and communality of the knowledge of the person of Jesus Christ as the centre of the *gospel* can be none other than that of the God-awakened *faith*. Critical–historical study signifies the deserved and necessary end of those 'foundations' of this knowledge which are no foundations at all since they have not been laid by God Himself. Whoever does not yet know that we *no* longer know Christ according to the flesh, should let the critical study of the bible tell him so. The more radically he is frightened the better it is for him and for the matter involved. This might turn out to be the service which 'historical knowledge' can render to the actual task of theology.

15. If theology were to regain the courage to face up to concrete objectivity, the courage to bear witness to the *Word* of revelation, of judgement and *God's* love, the outcome might well be that 'science in general' would have to seek 'strong ties and a blood-relationship' with theology instead of the other way around; for it would be better perhaps also for jurists, physicians and philosophers if they knew what theologians ought to know. Or should the present fortuitous *opinio communis* of others really be the instance through which we have to let our work be judged as to its 'persuasiveness and value'?[27]

So Barth answered Harnack. Understanding the Bible is a work of the Holy Spirit and cannot be achieved through any human abilities or methods. Only faith as a gift of God can show us the real Jesus. All that historical criticism can show us is that the real Jesus is impossible to know on historical–critical grounds. That is the only use of such methods. Finally, if theology would take the objectivity of God's revelation seriously, then it is science that would have to seek validation, not the other way round. Theology must be the judge of critical science. The current opinions of the scientific and critical community can never judge the word of God. Barth even said that the knowledge of God was about being born again rather than any development of human thought. As far as Barth is concerned, the credibility of the Bible cannot be established by any human methods at all. Only the Holy Spirit can do this. In saying this, Barth is doing nothing more than repeating what Calvin had said in the *Institutes* – only Barth says it more politely.

Although many of Barth's disciples attempted to implement what he described, by and large their efforts have been little more than a combination of the two theologies of Barth and Harnack. In fact, Brevard Childs himself argues that the radical voice of theological dissent, led by Barth in the 1920s and 1930s, had become considerably domesticated by the 1940s.[28] This lapse back into the easy academic slumber of historical–critical methods has gone on too long.

Robert Jenson puts his finger on a key issue. The real problem with the practice of the critical method was the maintenance of historical distance.

There is a vast span of history between Julius Caesar and Bill Clinton. For premodern societies such time separation is exactly what binds persons and events together in a common world, so that Clinton might well read the Gallic Wars for help with his current problems, on the assumption that both he and Caesar are in the business of politics. *Modernity's* 'historical consciousness' experiences that time as a *separation*, so that Clinton and Caesar are each in their own historical world and the possibility of Caesar advising Clinton is problematic. Historical consciousness, which is the dynamic at the heart of historical–critical reading, *keeps historical distance...*[29]

Jenson is not alone in finding this fault. Remember how for Lessing the world of the Bible is not the world of the eighteenth century? As long as we sustain Lessing's sense of historical distance, the point of the Bible remains hidden. When the Bible tells us about what once happened, it does so in the knowledge that the readers, whether they live in 1000BCE or in 2000CE, share the same reality, lives in the same world. If I may be permitted to quote the blessed Barth one last time, the opening words of the preface to the first edition of his mighty commentary on Romans are these:

> Paul, as a child of his age, addressed his contemporaries. It is, however, far more important that, as Prophet and Apostle of the Kingdom of God, he veritably speaks to all men of every age. The differences between then and now, there and here, no doubt require careful investigation and consideration. But the purpose of such investigation can only be to demonstrate that these differences are, in fact, purely trivial.[30]

The modern paradigm of (even 'Evangelical') biblical scholarship has for too long adopted the historical–critical paradigms. A commentary would tell us lots about the commentator's reconstruction of ancient Semitic burial practices, or a suggested temple worship setting for a psalm, or the role of female gladiators in first-century Corinthian hat-making. But what we will *not* get is a serious engagement with the truths set forth in the Bible.

For too long Old Testament scholarship has been dominated by Yahwistic Unitarianism. It is time for us to read the Bible in the way that it was given to be read. In the gospels, Jesus actually imagines that anyone who read the Old Testament properly would be a Christian, a person who recognized Jesus as the Lord God of Israel.

The Reformers knew that unless the Bible was set free from the magisterium of the church, then its freedom and authority could never be experienced within the church. The Bible is not only our sole authority, but it is also clear and accessible to any and every Christian who reads it with faith and humility.

One of the great achievements of the Reformation was to put the Bible into the hands of every member of the congregation. The idea that only the church's experts, the magisterium, were competent to interpret the Bible was recognized for the deadly heresy that it is.

Nevertheless, the danger of the new 'Evangelical' magisterium needs to be recognized. The great hope of interpreting the Bible biblically is that it recovers the truth of the perspicuity of Scripture – and perhaps this is the most needed doctrine for our day. It has become commonplace to hear members of the congregation say things like 'I can't interpret the Bible because I haven't been to Bible college.'

This feeling of impotence in Bible reading does not come about by accident. Too often 'Evangelical' exegesis finds its meaning not so much in the text, but in historically reconstructed circumstances that are alleged to have been the setting for the original writing.

We live in interesting times. The empire of historical criticism is being challenged not only by pagan postmodernists, but also by the faithful church, which wants to find ways out of its Babylonian captivity. The recognition that without the Holy Spirit the Bible is a closed book is beginning to dawn. It may well be that, as in the 1940s, the church will succumb once again to the easy slumber of critical and hermeneutical studies (but pray God that it won't). Pray also that we will see the day when an evangelical church nourished by nothing but the perspicuous word of God will take its stand for the impossible possibility of the gospel in an increasingly pagan world.

*   *   *

Paul Blackham is Associate Minister (Theology) at All Soul's, Langham Place, London. His doctorate was on the doctrine of the Holy Spirit in Puritan theology.

Notes

1 *Weimar Ausgabe* (WA) 10ii, 73; Luther's Works (LW) 35, 132. (The standard reference procedure for Luther is to quote the accepted German edition, the *Weimar Ausgabe* (WA), as well as the English translation, *Luther's Works* (LW), published by Concordia Publishing House, St Louis, Missouri.)

2 *WA* 46, 414.

3 *WA* 10iii, 238.

4 *WA* 10,^{1,2}, 6.

5 *WA* 8,69; LW 32, 176.

6 Paul Althaus, *The Theology of Martin Luther* (Philadelphia: Fortress Press, 1966), p. 77.

7 Ibid. p. 78.

8 John Calvin, *Institutes of the Christian Religion* I.5.11. All translations are from John Calvin, *Institutes of the Christian Religion*, J.T. McNeill (ed.) F.L. Battles (tr.) (London: SCM, 1960).

9 Ibid. I.5.11.

10 Ibid. I.6.1.

11 Ibid. I.6.3.

12 Ibid. II.6.2.

13 Ibid. I.7.1–2

14 Ibid. I.7.4.

15 Ibid. I.7.5.

16 Ibid. II.2.20.

17 Ibid. II.2.21.

18 John Calvin, *Calvin Commentaries: Galatians, Ephesians, Philippians and Colossians*, T.H.L. Parker (tr.) (Edinburgh and London: Oliver and Boyd, 1965), p. 85.

19 E.A. Dowey, *The Knowledge of God in Calvin's Theology* (New York: Columbia University Press, 1952), p. 162.

20 Klaus Scholder, *The Birth of Modern Critical Theology: Origins and Problems of Biblical Criticism in the Seventeenth Century* (London: SCM, 1990).

21 K. Barth, *Church Dogmatics* I.2, T.F. Torrance and G.W. Bromiley (trs) (Edinburgh: T&T Clark, 1956), p. 4.

22 Reimarus worked on a study of Jesus that was only published after his death by Lessing. He considered Jesus solely from the

standpoint of general history; that is, he treated Him not as Saviour and Son of God, but just as any other historical figure and with the same criteria. In doing so, he treated Scripture not as the inspired word of God, but just like any other historical text and with the same criteria. Lessing championed Reimarus' historical–critical approach, which has, since the eighteenth century, gained ground in both academy and church.

23 H. Chadwick (ed.), *Lessing's Theological Writings* (London: A&C Black, 1956), p. 18.

24 Ibid. p. 52.

25 Adolf von Harnack was one of the greatest liberal Protestant theologians of the late nineteenth and early twentieth centuries. Karl Barth's theological career from the time of his commentary on Romans of 1919 was marked by a radical protest against the sort of Christianity and theology Harnack both advocated and represented. It was no surprise that Harnack gave some critical responses to Barth's project, which received no less critical replies from Barth himself. Public correspondence between the two theologians took place in the early 1920s.

26 H. Martin Rumscheidt, *Revelation and Theology: An Analysis of the Barth–Harnack Correspondence of 1923* (Cambridge: Cambridge University Press, 1972), pp. 29–31.

27 Ibid. pp. .32–5.

28 C. Braaten and R. W. Jenson (eds.), *Reclaiming the Bible for the Church* (Edinburgh: T&T Clark, 1995), p. 2.

29 Ibid. p. 103.

30 Karl Barth, *The Epistle to the Romans*, E.C. Hoskyns (tr.) (Oxford: Oxford University Press, 1933), p. 1.

7

Evangelicals and Preaching

Iain Taylor

The following pages offer three theses that provide some broad outlines of what it means for preaching to be properly evangelical. But first an observation.

Often in the 'Evangelical' churches one visits, one notices that when those who lead the churches lay great stress on the fact that the test of a good church is how good the preaching is, those in the pew (and presumably those at the front as well) assume that the preaching at *this* church is good enough to pass the test. They may be right, but if one is not already pre-disposed to join in this mutual back-patting, one might find less than adequate reasons offered for such confidence. Often one fails to encounter any argument for this view, although one often hears that at other churches they do not take the Bible all that seriously – again, often stated without being argued. But this is just to beg the question, the question we shall explore here.

Just what makes preaching good preaching? That is the key question for all who turn up either to give or to hear sermons every Sunday. And, in particular, it is the question that is rightly addressed but insufficiently answered by the situation just mentioned. Reasons that could be offered include the following: it takes the Bible seriously; it addresses the needs of the day for individuals, church and society; it offers medicine to the weary soul, enriching the emotions and affections. These are all good and proper reasons. But they are good and proper most of all when they are located within the realm of the gospel. When informed and constrained by the gospel, preaching can be truly biblical, truly relevant and truly therapeutic. There is no Spirit other than the Spirit of Jesus Christ, as the apostle Paul repeatedly stresses to the churches in his care (Galatians 3:1–5; 1 Corinthians 12:3, for example). And so when He does His work of illumining the words of Scripture, of speaking the word of truth into a world of falsehood and of speaking the word of comfort to the troubled soul, it will always be from, with and by means of, Christ and His gospel. And when these reasons are proffered with insufficient reference to the gospel framework, the correct desire for biblical faithfulness, contemporary relevance and affective therapy can become skewed. What is needed is preaching that is truly evangelical.

There is much that could be said here about the nature and task of evangelical preaching. The focus here will be on the effect on preaching of conceptions of the content and scope of the gospel. The tendencies of distortionism and reductionism that I outlined in the introduction have significant consequences on preaching, and we shall see how a true grasp of full gospel preaching can be truly faithful, relevant and therapeutic preaching.

1. Truly evangelical preaching is not a merely human activity or technique, and can never be mere human words or mere human ideas and opinions. Rather it is a spiritual discipline and as such it is bound to the Spirit's witness to Jesus Christ, His holiness and His freedom.

Preaching is a spiritual discipline

That is, it is the work of the Holy Spirit. It is not our work, message or performance. It is His. Or to put it better, it is our work, message and performance, but only because it is His first and only as it is enabled, liberated and commanded by Him. Otherwise, like the loveless martyr, it is as effective as a clanging gong or clashing cymbal. The great preacher is not a genius who demonstrates great reading and comes up with great ideas. The great preacher is not an entertainer who is armed with an array of illustrations, anecdotes and witty repartee that can spice up a talk on any topic whatsoever. And the great preacher is not a virtuoso whose personal charisma and sheer brilliance can lead and motivate the most apparently resistant of congregations.

No matter how full the churches of the genius, entertainer or virtuoso may be, the gospel preacher is not to envy them. The gospel preacher is first of all a servant of the Spirit of Christ, and waits on Him for life and growth that is spiritual not earthly, namely, of the Holy Spirit, and not some profane one. It is He who quickens the preacher to be the mouthpiece of the very oracles of God. It is He who opens the hearts, ears and lives of the hearers to understand and obey the message. The same Holy Spirit that in an earlier age worked to fashion Scripture as a clear and effective witness to our Lord and Saviour Jesus Christ still works to quicken its words to testify to Jesus. Without His work sermons will be mere words that profit us nothing.

But what does this appeal to the Spirit mean? As a spiritual discipline, preaching will be focused on Jesus Christ, as we shall investigate more fully later. He is not just any spirit but the Spirit of Christ, who imparts to us and seals in our hearts not just any message, but the gospel of Christ's death and resurrection. As Christ says:

> When he, the Spirit of truth, comes, he will guide you into all truth. He will not speak on his own; he will speak only what he hears, and he will tell you what is yet to come. He will bring glory to me by taking from what is mine and making it known to you. All that belongs to the Father is mine. That is why I said the Spirit will take from what is mine and make it known to you.' (John 16:13–15)

As a spiritual discipline, preaching will be an act of holiness

He is not the spirit of moral and ethical indifference but the
Spirit of holiness and truth. As He works He will put to death
the sins of both preacher and hearer and clothe them with the
purity of Jesus Christ (Romans 8:9–13; Galatians 5:16–17).
Preaching therefore demands sanctification. It means the
preacher's holiness as his or her mind is fixed on the good
news, as his or her words are conformed to the content of the
message of Jesus and as his or her heart is enabled to wait on
the Spirit to give the obedience to what has been preached. It
also means the hearers' holiness as their hearts are opened to
receive the message of sin and grace, and as their wills are
quickened to live obediently. Holiness is a genuine mark of
spiritual preaching, and our sermons will only give rise to this
sanctification if the Spirit is at work. This is not to confuse the
success of a sermon by the personal piety of either preacher or
congregation, which has sometimes been the temptation of a
rather over-zealous pietism to which 'Evangelicals' have often
fallen prey. The Giver of Life is not holy people, but the Holy
Spirit. But the need for sanctification in preaching must not be
minimized. Evangelical preaching is required neither for
knowledge of the biblical text, nor to motivate the hearers, nor
for the entertainment of the congregation, nor to pep up the
people's spirits or restore their psychological equilibrium.
Evangelical preaching, rather, is that word of power, which by
the Spirit's work alone imparts salvation to God's people. It is
for knowledge of and obedience to Jesus Christ.

Evangelical preaching *will* provide the knowledge, motiva-
tion, therapy and relevance of all these other approaches, but
not in an unsanctified form. Its focus, like that of the Spirit,
will be to make us like Christ. Preaching, then, is not an intellectual exercise like an essay, a lecture or a college exegesis.
Nor is preaching a training session to motivate the hearers to
join in and attend the church activities so beloved of the
preacher. Nor is preaching a performance to amuse and
impress an expectant congregation who treat church like

consumers. Nor is preaching a therapy session that has to adapt to the 'needs' of the hearers by telling them what they feel they want to hear. There may be plenty of 'Evangelical' pastors who have let their sermons be dictated by these concerns, but their preaching may have ceased to be truly evangelical as a result. The evangelical preacher can eschew all these false expectations and get down to the simple but serious discipline of proclaiming Jesus as our Lord and Saviour in the power of the Spirit.

As a spiritual discipline, preaching will be an act of freedom

He is not the spirit of slavery but the Spirit of sonship. By His work we become not slaves but children of God. We become freed not just from sin but also from law. 'Now that faith has come', Paul writes, 'we are no longer under the supervision of the law ... if you are led by the Spirit you are not under law' (Galatians 3:25, 5:18). The shocking news that all of us, the most religious of us especially, have to learn about the gospel is that it is opposed to systems of rule keeping. This holds for preaching as well.

This freedom should not be misunderstood. True spiritual freedom is opposed neither to the Spirit's witness to Jesus Christ nor to His holiness. The arbitrary or capricious preacher that thinks he can dispense God's Spirit without giving glory to Christ and without His sanctifying work is no evangelical preacher. The Spirit does not set us free from Jesus Christ or from a holy life – He sets us free for them.

But this true freedom is nevertheless a real freedom and must be separated from the sort of rule keeping that is unfitting for those who have the Spirit. Evangelical preachers do not need to plagiarize others' talks to ensure they achieve the one true and sound exposition of the passage. They do not need a stock of witty jokes or funny stories. What they need to do is to keep in step with the Spirit, the very Spirit who will guide us into the truth of Christ and who will conform us and our churches to Christ's holiness. We should be grateful for all the useful advice that others may give us. We should make use of all the latest wisdom on preaching techniques. We should listen to those around us who tell us insistently what they want us to preach and how. But the gospel preacher is free from all this. He or she is free in relation to the church and to the world – even free in how to preach.

Evangelical preachers are free from and for their congregation. They are bound to the Lord of the church, and only as such can they serve their congregations. The are not to be bound by the agendas of the PCC, eldership, diaconate and church meeting. They are not to be bound by the demands of the most vociferous of church members. They are to listen obediently to their Lord and to wait on His Spirit. But as they listen to the Lord of the church, they will necessarily be moved to serve the church He bought with His blood.

Evangelical preachers are free from and for the world around them. They are not to be bound to the agenda of the academy or the newspaper. They are not bound to preach what is acceptable to the élite of society. They are not bound to justify the ignorance and prejudices of those around them. They are not to be bound to the manifesto of any political party. What matters in preaching is the Spirit of Christ rather than the spirit of the world, and it is He that we must keep in step with and listen to, rather than the winds of fashion. But as they are obedient to the Lord of all the earth, they will reflect His deep longing for the needs and pain of all His creation.

Evangelical preachers are free from and for rules about how to preach. The gospel preacher is not to be bound by any particular form of topical or expository preaching. They are not to be bound by any particular doctrinal formulae or by any church's subcultural traditions, no matter how 'Evangelical' their pedigree. And they are not to be bound by any oratorical techniques about how to communicate effectively in the modern or postmodern age. Gospel preachers are free from all this, and are subject only to the Spirit whose coming has brought the age of law to an end. But as they are led by the Spirit who has guided others before them in the path of Christ, they will seek to learn the wisdom of their fellow travellers.

2. Biblical preaching is not talking about the Bible. Biblical preaching is talking about what the Bible talks about – that is, it must be focused on the gospel of Jesus Christ.

What does the Bible talk about? The Bible talks about Jesus. He himself says so. Against the Jews in John's gospel He says, 'You search the scriptures because you think that in them you have eternal life; and it is they that testify on my behalf. Yet you refuse to come to me to have life' (John 5:39–40). It is the message of the prophets: 'The prophets who prophesied of the grace that was to be yours made careful search and inquiry, inquiring about the person or time that the Spirit of Christ within them indicated when it testified in advance to the sufferings destined for Christ and the subsequent glory' (1 Peter 1:10–11). It is the message of the apostles: 'You Israelites, listen to what I have to say: Jesus of Nazareth... ' (Acts 2:22). It is the sum total of the gospel: 'Paul... set apart for the gospel of God... the gospel concerning his Son... [who is] Jesus Christ our Lord' (Romans 1:1–4).

Jesus is God's very Word, the One – the only One – who has made God known to us. Jesus is the origin, centre and destiny of all things; in Him is to be found the meaning of all things, since 'all things were created by him and for him. He is before all things, and in him all things hold together' (Colossians 1:16–17). Jesus is our sole and sufficient salvation. That there is no other Saviour, help or comfort for us in life or in death, which need not perplex us or lead us to despair, since as the One who puts all things right, all our needs and wants find their sole but also total answer in Him. 'For God was pleased to have all his fullness dwell in him, and through him to reconcile to himself all things, whether things on earth or things in heaven, by making peace through his blood shed on the cross' (Colossians 1:19–20). In short, Jesus is all that God has to say.

How, then, can truly evangelical preaching be fundamentally about anything else? If Jesus Christ as God's one Word is all that He has to say, must not preaching, if it too seeks to be God's Word, be dominated by this one theme?

To some it might seem otherwise. Perhaps someone will object that basically there are other things that one has to include in preaching. 'What about the Bible?' one might say. 'It talks about many more things than just Jesus. What about the creation, heaven and hell, the Spirit, the moral law and a whole host of other things?' But it is the clear witness of Scripture that to read Scripture and not to be confronted with Jesus Christ is unspiritual and to have missed the point. Talk about these things apart from Christ and you are talking about their corrupt, sinful, unreconciled, and therefore *unbiblical* form. Do this, and one risks talking about the Bible as if what it says – that is, that Christ is the inescapable centre and destiny of all things – is not true.

So then, to answer the objection 'What about the Bible?' Whatever you think the Bible is talking about, if it does not find its central significance in Jesus Christ, then your reading is at odds with gospel reality. The Bible contains many words, but its heart and focus, without which all those other words are without meaning or life, is the one Word and name 'Jesus Christ'.

'What about the needs of the congregation?' one might say. 'People need more than just the message of Jesus saving us from sin, absolutely essential though that is. We need to live for God in the world today. We have to deal with issues of family life, of how to serve God at work and in society at large. We have to address the emotional, psychological and intellectual issues Christians face if they are to live effectively for God. For a healthy and growing church, we really have to talk about much more than that same old message of Jesus and the cross.' But all things are really in Jesus Christ, and needed to be put to death with Him on the cross and raised with Him in His resurrection to be reconciled to God. Talk about these things apart from Christ and you are talking about their corrupt, sinful, unreconciled and therefore *pastorally dangerous* form. On this path one runs the danger of the pastoral fallout that inevitably comes from relying on the world and from building one's house on sand rather than the rock that is Jesus Christ.

So then, to answer the objection: 'What about the needs of the congregation?' Whatever you think your congregation needs to hear, whether it is a matter of the head, heart or soul, it needs to hear about Jesus Christ. All those good things you want to share with your hearers are only good in, through and because of Him. All good things come from Him, all good things have their meaning and focus in Him, and all good things require the transformation they achieved by being reconciled to God by Christ's death and resurrection. And do not both these objections by their very nature betray the belief in a Christ who is denuded of His true gospel fullness?

This is the key test of a biblical preaching ministry: how much is Jesus talked about? Like the apostles, 'We proclaim Him.'

Without doubt we all fail in many ways as preachers and our sermons are littered with instances of individual distortions and reductions. As if any sermon could do complete justice to the mystery of God's love for us, let alone when the sermon is delivered by a frail and sinful creature! But when there is a chronic inability to understand Jesus in all His gospel fullness, whether from fundamental distortion or reduction – that is, where the preacher is so tied to a particular conception of the gospel that when faced with the witness of Scripture he or she seems incapable of seeing the discrepancy – a preaching ministry will fall short of its evangelical standard. Earlier we showed how this can happen in general terms by what we called distortionism and reductionism.

There is a form of distortionism at work when preaching tends to the danger of proclaiming a Jesus that is the invention of the preacher or that sits loose to the text of Scripture. It is hoped that what we have said already will have made it clear how such a preaching strategy, if followed consistently, cannot claim spiritual support. We proclaim not just any Christ but the Christ of the prophets and apostles.

But there is also a form of reductionism that for all its talk about the Bible can be rather reticent on what the Bible actually talks about, that is Christ and His gospel. Evangelical preaching cannot be this false fidelity to Scripture that concerns itself endlessly with the details of its textual form without grappling seriously with its gospel content.

This is most exemplified by sermons, commonly on the Old Testament, that never mention Jesus at all. But there are other ways in which biblical preaching can become more of a form than a content, against which the evangelical preacher should be on guard. Sometimes this can arise from an undue focus on the Bible as a series of character studies, or a training manual or a source of historical information. But it can also arise from the current emphasis in many Evangelical churches which I have heard termed SCEOTS (Systematic Consecutive Exposition Of The Scriptures). The correct intention lying behind this is that of expounding the whole counsel of God: this means teaching, if not every chapter and verse of Scripture, then at least every book within it. And as a rule it will go through each biblical book sequentially, chapter by chapter. Of course the evangelical preacher is not obliged to preach in this way, but as a method it has much to commend it. If one perpetually closes one's eyes to one part of Scripture one might miss out on a particular dimension of the fullness of gospel reality it has to show us.

However, without the rigorous focus on the centre of the gospel, that is Jesus Christ Himself, some of the good intentions can be undone. Without its true meaning and life-giving centre, that is Jesus, any explanation of Scripture runs the risk of being a well-presented and learned introductory-level talk on historical literature. It can be a perhaps very skilful talk on a set of rather uninteresting texts of a relatively obscure ancient people. Without Jesus Christ it will not be evangelical or biblical preaching, no matter how much 'biblical' language is used or how much the 'text' is dissected or explained. And for all its historical and literary interest and for all the hours the preacher has put into the preparation, on a deep experiential and spiritual level it will be superficial, irrelevant and dull.

Evangelical preaching's first task is not to explain a text. It is to proclaim the biblical Christ. On the mount of transfiguration, God called out from heaven, 'This is my beloved Son. Hear Him!' And in our sermons we should. As Karl Barth has written:

> One can never say of a single part of the narrative, doctrine and proclamation of the New Testament, that in itself it is original or important or the object of the witness intended. Neither the ethics of the Sermon of the Mount nor the eschatology of Mk 13 and parallels, nor the healing of the blind, lame and possessed, nor the battle with the Pharisees and the Cleansing of the Temple, nor the statements of Pauline and Johannine metaphysics and mysticism (so far as there are any), nor love to God nor love to neighbour, nor the passion and death of Christ, nor the miraculous raising from the dead – nothing of all that has any value, inner importance or abstract significance of its own in the New Testament, apart from Jesus Christ being the subject of it all. His is the name in which it is all true and real, living and moving, by which, therefore, everything must be attested.[1]

3. Evangelical preaching is to be as particular, broad and relevant as is the gospel it is charged to proclaim.

Good preaching depends on rightly grasping the content and scope of the gospel. Preaching that is truly evangelical will take its primary cue neither from what is commonly perceived to be the need of the hour, nor from a tradition of 'Evangelical' norms. Evangelical preaching must be controlled by the gospel and so must reflect its particularity, breadth and relevance.

Particular

The particularity that is the mark of truly evangelical preaching is the confidence of the preacher that it really is the biblical message of Jesus Christ that will be the Spirit's chosen means of giving life to all. Evangelical preachers will want to speak as broadly and relevantly as the message of Scripture and the needs of their community dictate. But they will do so in the certainty that the answers to those needs are to be found in the source of all wisdom and knowledge, namely Jesus Christ. Their sermons will therefore always have their centre in Him, in terms of both content and trajectory. The preacher, that is, is the herald of the good news that all things have been reconciled in Jesus Christ.

This is an extension of what we have discussed above, but it also has significant implications for the way the preacher goes about preparing the sermon. The particularity of the message for the evangelical preacher means that there is a clear focus to his or her work. The preacher does not need to read voraciously outside the Bible to find what to say. Nor does he or she need to be concerned about any and every question people may have about what is in the Bible. Evangelical preachers can be confident that all their congregation's needs and all the mysteries of scriptural exegesis find their resolution in the piercing and rich simplicity of the biblical Christ. Preaching is not easy, since it is not a human but a spiritual possibility. But it is simple, since it deals solely with the simple reality that in Jesus Christ God has said and done all that He needs to.

Some words from James S. Stewart make this point excellently.

'We preach always Him,' declared Luther, 'the true God and man. This may seem a limited and monotonous subject, likely to be soon exhausted, but we are never at the end of it.' Why should you imagine that the stimulating atmosphere of expectation which surrounds you at the opening of your ministry must inevitably give way sooner or later to a sultry air of tedious disenchantment? Does spring, regularly returning year by year, ever become monotonous? Is not its wonder as fresh and unspoilt still as when the morning stars sang together and the sons of God shouted for joy? And are God's mighty acts in history and redemption less enthralling than His mighty acts in nature? Drop dogma [doctrine about Jesus Christ] from your preaching, and for a brief time you may titillate the fancy of the superficial, and have them talking about your cleverness; but that type of ministry wears out speedily, and garners no spiritual harvest in the end. Therefore settle it with your own souls now that, whatever else you may do or leave undone, you will preach in season and out of season God's redemptive deed in Christ.[2]

Broad

The breadth that is the mark of truly evangelical preaching is the preacher's confidence that by the biblical message of Jesus Christ the Spirit will really give life to all. Evangelical preachers will not shy away from speaking as broadly and relevantly as the message of Scripture and the needs of their community dictate. They do this because they know that, no matter how insignificant and peripheral the figure of Jesus of Nazareth might appear, His gospel is a word of power that transforms all of creation. The preacher is the herald of the good news that in Jesus Christ all things have been reconciled.

There is, then, no limit to the range of the Jesus-centred sermon. There is not one passage of Scripture, there is not one church situation, there is not one social problem, there is not one political issue, there is not one world event, there is not one personal need, there is not one individual joy or crisis, there is not one moral dilemma that does not come under the purview of Christ and His gospel and that does not need the illumination and healing balm that come from Him alone.

Again, one has to resist the temptation of explaining this in such a way that turns sermons into performances and preachers into genii or virtuosi. There is the wrong sort of 'Evangelical' preacher who ranges about, widely touching on many topics, but seldom touching base with the gospel of the Christ of Scripture.

But although it is true that by firing in any direction whatever one is less likely to hit the target, it is also true that a narrowness of vision that fails to see the whole target can leave enemy strongholds intact. It has to be admitted that there is the sort of preacher who, whatever the text or occasion, has only one sermon. Thankfully they are rare, and thankfully their sermons are invariably good ones and are worth a second hearing. But there are also some 'Evangelical' preachers, who despite their obvious gifts in clear thought and expression and their genuine concern for biblical truth, may have their own blindspots that come from too zealous an emphasis on the orthodoxy of an 'Evangelical' tradition. And this may be more than the sort of overemphasis of one particular model of the atonement that flattens out the richer and more nuanced contours of what the Bible says.

For instance it is common to hear in 'Evangelical' churches – even on the lips of preachers who not only are intelligent and well-educated, but also have put hours of study into biblical commentaries – sermons that, whatever the text, struggle to go beyond a mere handful of applications. Often these include (and can almost be exhausted by) the following: have a 'quiet time' of personal Bible reading and prayer; don't date a non-Christian; don't get drunk or sleep around; invite your friends to evangelistic events; turn up to church meetings. And when congregations are exhorted to lives of love, it will not do to encourage church members just to be nicer to each other. As someone once said, 'Even "sinners" do that' (Luke 6:33). Biblical, evangelical Christianity requires more, and preaching must reflect this richer life to which Christ has called us.

But there are also more subtle cases. Here is a striking example of how – in this case – a very adept church leader can go awry in explaining Scripture when he or she is captive to a reduced notion of the gospel. It was given as a ten-minute introduction to a prayer meeting and was meant to be an encouragement to spur on and guide our prayers.

The leader spoke on Jesus' words at the end of his High Priestly Prayer in John 17:20–24:

> My prayer is not for them alone. I pray also for those who will believe in me through their message, that all of them may be one, Father, just as you are in me and I am in you. May they also be in us so that the world may believe that you have sent me. I have given them the glory that you gave me, that they may be

one as we are one: I in them and you in me. May they
be brought to complete unity to let the world know that you
sent me and have loved them even as you have loved me.

For whatever reason – probably ecclesiastical isolationism –
the speaker chose not to focus on the main point of the passage, which is that Jesus wants his people to be at one. His
main stress was on the point that Jesus was not intending here:
the sort of unity that had little concern for the truth content of
the message. Of course it is correct, as he emphasized, that
godly unity is on the basis of evangelical truth.[3] But he then
went on to say that the message for us was not to work for a
false unity, but to resist such attempts in defence of the gospel,
the true source of unity. And the prayers that followed were
quite clearly against any form of ecumenical rapprochement.

To explain the passage and to pray through it in that way
seemed plausible to the group of people present, a group that
included many mature and adept Bible teachers. The irony is,
however, that, for all the biblical knowledge of the speaker
and hearers in that meeting, the people in the meeting started
praying in ways that go against Jesus' prayer, the very prayer
the speaker had been explaining. And this is not an isolated
example. It is not just a fact of getting an individual text wrong
– such a thing would be regrettable, but not a serious problem.
The problem here is that the speaker was bound to a particular understanding of what it meant to be a gospel church, a
reduced form that ended up distorting its message to such an
extent that on a very uncharitable reading one could say he
contradicted the very thrust of the passage with a carefree air.

The models of preaching that encourage a reading and exposition of all the Scriptures are to be commended lest as preachers
and congregations we miss out on the whole counsel of God.
Nevertheless, when this right concern for biblical faithfulness is
allied to a fairly certain notion of what the gospel is that is still
bound to a reduced form, the whole counsel of God will not be
preached even if you were to preach through the whole Bible
chapter by chapter. So, for instance, if one has a tendency to see

God's church and work as restricted to a particular confession
and has a relatively cool attitude to the broader church, Jesus'
words in John 17 ought to give one cause to think again. But if
one reads them and even explains them in a way that reinforces
ecclesiastical separation and even gets people praying against
perhaps faithful and obedient attempts to live in the light of
what Christ wants for us, something must have gone wrong.
One should seek to preach Christ in all the Scriptures, but if in
the Scriptures one is restricting oneself only to explaining a par-
tial Christ, how can even the most systematic and consecutive
expository preaching hope to present the full biblical Christ?

Relevant

The gospel is not a bare word. It is a word addressed *to* someone. It is a word addressed to *us*. God speaks to us in the
gospel in a powerful, arresting and relevant way. It is powerful because it is His word. It is arresting because it is about the
most serious matter of life and death. And it is relevant
because it is about our life and death. As it is written, 'The
word of God is living and active. Sharper than any two-edged
sword, it penetrates even to dividing soul and spirit, joints and
marrow' (Hebrews 4:12).

God has *already* come near to us in Jesus Christ. The gospel,
therefore, is already relevant to us. It does not need to be made
so. It is God's very word of power, and so is glorious and radi-
ant in itself.

This truth has implications for the issue of the sermon's
application. If the gospel is already relevant to us, and if the
gospel is already an all-sufficient word of life, why should it
need a helping hand if it is to have an effect on our lives?
God's word is sufficient and His Spirit is powerful.

This is not to say that it has the sort of relevance that all of
us might want. For instance, although it is clear that in some
real sense all things have their meaning in Jesus Christ, this is
more straightforwardly apparent for some things than for
others – and on some matters Scripture may keep silent. And
when it does say something clear and direct, we might find it

so repulsive that we try our best to distance ourselves from it
– sometimes its very relevance is the thing we do not want.
And the focus of this gospel relevance is very specific:
Scripture is primarily concerned with our salvation in Jesus
Christ.

But this is nevertheless a true and genuine relevance, a relevance that affects all that Christ came to save, and so a relevance
to all of our lives. The application of the sermon, if it is determined
by the relevance of the gospel of Jesus Christ, will necessarily
come from the heart of the message, and this will be true and life-
giving.

Nevertheless, there are at least two ways in which this gospel
relevance may be compromised. The first is when the gospel
seems weak and irrelevant because it is not the full gospel that
is being preached. This may happen in many ways, such as
when the gospel is seen as the message of forgiveness of sins
and not as directions for life. It may also happen when preaching is seen as the dissection of an ancient text that is cut off
from the immediacy of its living gospel context. The Bible may
well have been a word to someone else then, but it does not
seem to be God's word to me now.

It may be that this explains some of the relatively high drop-
out rate there is among 'Evangelical' converts. There are no
doubt some who become disenchanted with the gospel the
church presents to them for reasons of unbelief and sin. But
there are many who become disillusioned because they cannot
see how it is relevant to their own lives. The gospel is made to
seem disconnected from real life, to be about some other world
and not this one. It is not surprising, therefore, if people feel
they need to look elsewhere than the gospel to find out about
life in the real world. But this should not be, since the rich fare
of the full gospel is more satisfying than the thin gruel that is
sometimes served up. Dave Tomlinson highlights this point
vividly when he recalls the words of the son of a leading
churchman, who said to his father: 'That man [the preacher] is
saying all of the right things, but he isn't saying them to anybody. He doesn't know where I am, and it would never occur

to him to ask!'[4] But this can only be half right (and not because there aren't many irrelevant preachers!). As a gospel preacher one cannot say *all* the right things and be irrelevant. If your preaching ministry is irrelevant, that is because you are at best saying only *some* of the right things, and need to say a lot more if you are to be faithful to the breadth and power of the gospel.

The second threat to the gospel's relevance is when there is a real and powerful application in the sermon but it does not come from the gospel. That is, there is a tendency to assume that the gospel, for all its truth, is somehow irrelevant in itself and needs to be made relevant by something else. This is perhaps most obvious when the Bible is seen as a collection of phrases and ideas that can serve as a springboard to talk instead about something that seems more interesting to both preacher and congregation whose basis in the gospel is incidental. The gospel can then become a good way of talking about something else, whereas it is the gospel itself that preachers should be talking about.

But this tendency of thinking that the biblical gospel needs to be made relevant by something else does commonly take on a more subtle and sophisticated form. In the last couple of decades in particular there has been an increasing interest within the 'Evangelical' constituency in the discipline of hermeneutics. This springs undeniably from the laudable desires to take the Bible seriously and to apply it to the contemporary world, and may in practice be sometimes not only benign but also positively helpful and enlightening for truly evangelical preaching. But there are also real dangers associated with hermeneutics, which should cause those who seek to be evangelical to be wary. Hermeneutics, if it is not disciplined by the gospel, can undermine the real relevance of the gospel, and hence the vitality of gospel preaching.

The discipline of hermeneutics is a peculiarly modern invention. Often people think that the word 'hermeneutics' simply means the interpretation of Scripture. But this is not strictly accurate and obscures some very important distinctions. Hermeneutics is not synonymous with biblical interpretation. Rather, hermeneutics is not the interpretation, but the *theory* of interpretation or interpretations. More precisely, it is an *independent* theory of interpretation. And hermeneutics is a peculiarly modern invention since, although there has been biblical interpretation as long as their has been a community of faith, it has only been in the last few centuries that some have thought that one requires the existence of an independent discipline of philosophical hermeneutics to fulfil this task.

But it has to be asked whether a truly evangelical outlook can pay deference to such a discipline of hermeneutics with good conscience.[5] The existence of such a discipline and its necessity in interpreting Scripture might sit easily with certain doctrines of Scripture and certain understandings of how God communicates Himself, but, arguably, not with evangelical ones. A truly evangelical outlook cannot allow anything – and this includes a general theory of authorial intent, a general notion of 'worldviews' and the wrong sort of 'biblical theology' – to sit independently from the power of the gospel. Hermeneutics too, like all else, must come under the sway of the gospel, and submit to its purifying and life-giving discipline. Maybe after it has undergone its gospel discipline the study of hermeneutics can indeed be retained as a genuinely *evangelical* hermeneutics. But does not the assertion of the need for this and other bridging devices betray the assumption that the biblical gospel as it stands is rather lacking in relevance?

Conclusion

The preacher whose sole teacher is the Holy Spirit and whose sole theme is Jesus Christ will be an evangelical preacher. Such a preacher will be both faithful and relevant, will be both biblical and therapeutic, will appeal to both head and heart, and will speak forcefully to both church and world. Why? Because the gospel of Jesus Christ is that rich and that powerful and that satisfying.

There is no need, therefore, not to follow the apostle Paul who spoke 'not in words taught by human wisdom but by the

Spirit' (1 Corinthians 2:13), and in his preaching 'decided to know nothing... except Jesus Christ and him crucified' (v. 2). As Calvin says:

> We see that our whole salvation and all its parts are compre-hended in Christ. We should therefore take care not to derive the least portion of it from anywhere else. If we seek salvation, we are taught by the very name of Jesus that it is of him. If we seek any other gifts of the Spirit, they will be found in his anointing. If we seek strength, it lies in his dominion; if purity, in his conception; if gentleness, it appears at his birth. For by his birth he was made like us in all respects that he might learn to feel our pain. If we seek redemption, it lies in his passion; if acquittal, in his condemnation; if remission of the curse, in his cross; if satisfaction, in his sacrifice; if purification, in his blood; if reconciliation, in his descent into hell; if mortification of the flesh, in his tomb; if newness of life, in his resurrection; if immortality, in the same; if inheritance of the Heavenly Kingdom, in his entrance into heaven; if protection, if security, if abundant supply of all blessings, in His kingdom; if untrou-bled expectation of judgement, in the power given him to judge. In short, since such rich store of every kind of good abounds in him, let us drink our fill from this fountain, and from no other.[6]

* * *

Iain Taylor used to work at a church in West London and is currently pursuing doctoral research in Christian doctrine.

Notes

1 K. Barth, *Church Dogmatics* 1.2 (Edinburgh: T&T Clark, 1956), pp. 10–11. Calvin concurs. He writes in *Opera* 9.825:

The Scripture is not given us to satisfy our foolish curiosity or to serve our ambition. But it is useful St. Paul tells us; and why?

To teach us good doctrine, to console us, exhort us and render us perfect in every good work. So to that use let us put it. If we are asked: what is all this edification that we ought to receive from it, the answer, in a word, is that we learn thereby to put our trust in God and to walk in fear of him. And, inasmuch as Jesus Christ is the fulfilment of the Law and the Prophets and is the substance of the Gospel, that we incline towards no other end but to know him.

2 J.S. Stewart, *Heralds of God* (London: Hodder & Stoughton, 1946), pp. 68–9.

3 But might he have meant only 'Evangelical' truth?

4 D. Tomlinson, *The Post-evangelical* (London: Triangle, 1995), p. 140.

5 Not to mention the apparently less than consistent claim of some advocates of the necessity of this independent hermeneutics that it is compatible with the Reformation maxim of *sola scriptura*.

6 John Calvin *Institutes of the Christian Religion*, J.T. McNeill (ed.) F.L. Battles (tr.) (London: SCM, 1960), 2.16.19.

8

Evangelicals and Evangelism

Paul Weston

It was Canon Ted Wickham who concluded in his classic study of the church's impact on the industrial city of Sheffield in the nineteenth and early twentieth centuries that:

> Too often the gospel is preached wide outside the context of man's life in this world, thrown to him from outside like a lifebuoy (or even a brick) inscribed with a soteriological text that is meaningless to the secular mind and indifferent to the social context in which men are rooted.[1]

Wickham's words would find parallels in many eras of the church's life, not least our own. That his words applied to an era in which England was considered a far more 'Christianized' country than it is now (with the 'vocabulary' and conceptual apparatus necessary for making at least some sort of meaningful response to the language of Christian belief) is significant in itself. But the contemporary alienation of our culture from many of these remaining vestiges of Christendom has served to compound the problems associated with the task of contemporary Christian communication.

Two particular factors have contributed to this current dilemma. First, the rapid decline in church membership over the last fifty years is removing the significance of Christian words from meaningful intellectual and behavioural associations. The Church of England report entitled *All God's Children?: Children's Evangelism in Crisis*[2] indicated that of 2,000 listeners to the Daily Service in 1955, 83 per cent of people over the age of 16 claimed to have attended Sunday school or Bible class for several years in their childhood. Even if this figure is drastically reduced, owing to the unrepresentative nature of the sample, it still suggests that two-thirds of the adult population in the 1930s and 1940s regularly attended some sort of organized Sunday school. By contrast, the 1989 *English Church Census* showed that only 14 per cent of children under the age of 15 participated in any form of church-related activity on Sundays.[3] That figure is presently still on the decline and this looks set to continue.[4]

Second, the sweep of cultural change that has loosely been described as 'postmodernity' has served to diversify and dilute still further the plausibility of classical Christian belief. As Walter Truett Anderson puts it, 'In recent decades we have passed, like Alice slipping through the looking glass, into a new world.'[5] One aspect of this new world is that the older 'grand narratives' like Christianity can no longer be trusted to shape or give meaning to the totality of human experience. Instead, they are often viewed with intense suspicion. As Terry Eagleton writes:

> Post-modernism signals the death of such 'metanarratives' whose secretly terroristic function was to ground and legitimate the illusion of a 'universal' human history. We are now in the process of wakening from the nightmare of modernity, with its manipulative reason and fetish of the totality, into the laid-back pluralism of the post-modern, that heterogeneous range of life-styles and language games which has renounced the nostalgic urge to totalize and legitimate itself... Science and philosophy must jettison their grandiose metaphysical claims and view themselves more modestly as just another set of narratives.[6]

Loss of Confidence

As a result of these factors, many Christians are experiencing a loss of confidence in presenting the message of the gospel to their contemporaries, often struggling to make 'connections' between the gospel message they hear on a Sunday and the day-to-day lives of people they are trying to reach on Mondays to Saturdays. Attempts to say something evangelistic often come across as if from the mouth of an 'alien', somehow disconnected from the lives of those we try to reach.

In addition to this, it seems that ironically many evangelism training programmes have tended to accentuate rather than to diminish this communication 'gap'. Some suggest that we must fully understand the philosophy behind non-Christian worldviews before we can hope to engage with them, while others teach particular 'models' of gospel presentation that either rarely coincide with reality, or appear to supply 'spiritual' answers to questions that nobody is actually asking. All in all, these new realities of a post-Christian Britain confront the church with enormous communication challenges. As Mike Riddell concludes: 'The one massive gap in the church's expertise is *how to do mission in the post-Christian West.*'[7]

A return to the gospel(s)

There are unfortunately no easy answers or instant 'fixes' to these challenges, no handy 'how-to' kits on how to share the gospel in our contemporary post-Christian society. Nonetheless, in what follows I want to make some suggestions for further reflection and inquiry, which may help to stimulate fresh practice and confidence. My main contention is stunningly straightforward: that the time is ripe for a re-examination and re-appropriation of Jesus' spoken evangelistic methodology as recorded in the gospels. In developing this case I want to defend the notion that the idea of 'evangelism' is best understood as any process that allows Jesus to bear witness to Himself in His own words. I would argue that this approach has often been neglected in the past, but is very appropriate in engaging a postmodern 'story'-based culture, and therefore helps particularly to meet the apologetic needs of our generation.

Evangelism – then and now

If we examine the gospel 'tracts' or 'models' that have been in vogue in our evangelistic methodologies over the past several decades, we will find that the majority have taken the view that the best way to communicate the gospel is to synthesize or systematize the gospel message into a number of 'elements', 'principles' or 'propositions'. These 'summary' statements of the good news – whether it be the 'Four Spiritual Laws', the 'Bridge to Life', 'Knowing God Personally', or 'Two Ways to Live'[8] – are designed for easy memorization with a view to passing on to others. Evangelism takes place when these elements are communicated to non-believers.

I have no desire to dismiss these approaches, which have proved so useful to many in the past. My questions about them are raised in relation to their contemporary use as evangelistic tools. First, they tend to presuppose some grasp of Christian vocabulary in which concepts like 'creation', 'sin', 'wrath', 'judgement', 'atonement', 'salvation' and so on make some sort of sense. In addition they assume some degree of theological 'map' knowledge of how these doctrinal ideas fit together and relate to one another. Perhaps in a cultural context where there remained a residue of Christian vocabulary and understanding such presentations were at least partially meaningful. But my own experience is that they tend to start much too far down the line for most non-Christians, assuming some elementary grasp of Christian theology and vocabulary, which – as we have already noted – is becoming increasingly rare.

Second, I wonder whether this general approach to gospel presentation actually reflects biblical patterns of evangelism or whether in fact it tends to reverse them. Let me explain. Succinct statements of the gospel are certainly present within the New Testament. One thinks for example of Paul's summary of the identity of Jesus as Messiah in Romans 1:1–4, his overview of Jesus' saving work in 1 Corinthians 15:1–9, or his 'Hymn to Christ' in Philippians 2:5–11. In addition, the sermons recorded by Luke in Acts have (since the work of C.H. Dodd) been seen to follow a certain 'pattern' incorporating consistent elements in the presentation of the gospel.[9] Furthermore, the gospel writer John occasionally draws together his material in 'summary' form for the benefit of his readers.[10]

None the less, these examples of 'summary statements' can be shown not to be representative of normal patterns of evangelism. First, many of them appear in letters addressed primarily to Christians (as the examples in Romans, 1 Corinthians and Philippians demonstrate). Their function is to teach or to remind believers of the faith they have received so that they can remember it. Second, despite Dodd's work on the sermons in Acts, there appears to be a greater degree of flexibility in the presentation of the gospel in Acts than he allows. The desire to systematize these presentations has sometimes blurred the fact that both the cultural context of the audience and the questions raised by the different hearers appear to be more significant in the formulation of the sermons.[11] Third, the number of 'summary' statements in the gospels is sparse (and largely limited to the fourth Gospel). As Walter Hollenweger has written, 'one has to account for the fact that the four evangelists thought it vital to describe Jesus's evangelism *as a dialogical and situational approach*. There can be no doubt that they thought this approach essential to the content of the Good News.'[12]

Where summary statements do exist, they appear to function once more as teaching aids, summarizing and drawing together the foregoing material rather than as the basis for a methodology for communicating the gospel.[13]

One must be careful therefore not to overplay the existence of gospel 'summary' statements as providing an ongoing pattern for evangelistic proclamation. While a biblical theology undoubtedly provides the parameters for New

Testament evangelistic presentations, there is no evidence to suggest a rigid conformity in matters of content (or of presentation). Rather, the evidence suggests that gospel 'summaries' tended to be later and secondary developments to the primary and more relational modes of evangelistic engagement that are recorded. One might conclude therefore that many of our evangelistic aids reflect this secondary stage rather than the earlier and primary stage of dialogue and conversation.

I think it is possible to take this analysis a stage further also. For once the gospel is abstracted into a series of 'principles' or 'propositions', evangelism can often be taught as a process whereby one works *towards* such presentations. What tends to happen is that the 'system' is defended from 'without', either on grounds of its inherent 'reasonableness' (a very 'modern' idea), or on the basis of the accumulation of supporting evidence (be it historical, personal, or psychological). As a result many 'Evangelical' approaches to evangelism implicitly function on the basis that there exists some sort of 'common ground' between Christian and non-Christian upon which a defence and affirmation of Christianity can initially be constructed. 'Evidential' approaches to the historical fact of the resurrection, evidence for the existence of Jesus as a real historical figure, philosophical arguments for the validity of the miracles and so on are good examples of this kind of 'bridging' approach.[14] It assumes that during an 'evangelistic' conversation the evangelist is positioning himself or herself *outside* the framework of belief (that is, alongside the hearer) in order to persuade them to believe or investigate further on grounds that make sense to the non-believer's worldview.

'Outside-In' Evangelism

This style of approach to evangelism, with its accompanying framework of assumptions about evidence and apologetics, may be described as an 'outside-in' approach. It can be illustrated by the following diagram.

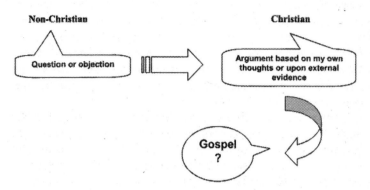

When a question is raised by a non-Christian, the evangelist seeks to work towards a presentation of the gospel either by means of his or her own opinions ('It's interesting you say that, I think that. . .'), or else by means of some form of rational supporting evidence ('There is actually enough good evidence for you to take Christianity seriously. . .'). What follows is usually a discussion about relative assumptions and presuppositions in which the evangelist's thinking is pitted more or less effectively against that of his or her hearer. To be sure, this method often stimulates the mind, but it rarely focuses upon the gospel. My own experience of this type of approach was one in which too much time was spent arguing around the philosophical and historical 'fringes' of the gospel while seldom actually reaching the point of explaining the good news itself.

'Inside-Out' Evangelism

Some years ago it was a revelation to me to spend time studying Jesus as an evangelist. The first thing I noticed was the fact that most of His evangelistic 'opportunities' arose out of ordinary conversations, often about quite secular and seemingly mundane concerns. For example, the sublime teaching on His identity as the One through whom men and women would worship God the Father 'in Spirit and in truth' begins with a simple request to a Samaritan woman for a drink on a hot day (John 4:7 ff.). Or again, in answer to a question about wealth and inheritance recorded in Luke 12:13, Jesus sidesteps the responsibility of arbitrating between the questioner and his brother (v. 14), and instead uses the opportunity to point up the folly of greed by telling the story of the 'rich fool' (vv. 16–21). In the light of the imminent coming of the kingdom, what is really needed is 'richness towards God' (v. 21). On another occasion a lawyer's question about 'who is my neighbour?' (Luke 10:29) prompts Jesus to tell the story we know as the 'Good Samaritan'. Once more a seemingly mundane question is taken as an opportunity to show that in the kingdom of God accepted thinking about family and 'bond' is radically re-orientated to include those considered to be racially impure and inferior (Luke 10:29–37). It is an illustration of Torah mercy rightly directed (v. 37).

A second thing I noticed was that in these encounters Jesus does not over-systematize His evangelistic message, nor does He appear to be working towards some sort of 'schematic' gospel presentation. Rather, He tackles questions as they arise and proceeds by addressing them in the light of the coming kingdom of God, shedding gospel light upon them and challenging hearers to respond in faith. In fact nearly all the stories and 'sermons' that we know so well from the gospels (and tend to isolate from their original settings) are initiated by specific questions and issues raised by sceptics and listeners in the course of Jesus' travelling ministry. They were not 'set piece' sermons prepared for formal religious occasions, but brilliant examples of Jesus' conversational evangelistic method in action. No question was outside the scope of the kingdom's relevance, for the kingdom of God was about the rightful rule of God over all matters, both secular and sacred.

A third thing I noticed was the number of times Jesus uses questions to deepen the level of the evangelistic dialogue. The actual statistics are striking. Matthew's gospel records ninety-four such questions on the lips of Jesus, Mark fifty-nine, Luke eighty-two and John forty-nine.[15] Questions can be used simply to illicit information, but the vast majority of Jesus' questions make His hearers reflect on what He has just said, or they invite the hearers to reflect on the words they themselves have spoken.[16]

Back to Jesus

I want to suggest that this represents an appropriate role model for contemporary evangelism. We need to train ourselves to 'inhabit' Jesus' kingdom worldview and to respond in corresponding ways to the impromptu questions of contemporary non-believers. How might this be done? I am not suggesting for one moment that we are able to imitate Jesus' technique and reproduce it. But what I am suggesting is that we train ourselves to use Jesus' own words in our evangelistic conversations, and that we pray for the divine insight and the Spirit's help to connect these words with contemporary questions. We take the gospel narratives as our material starting point and seek to find the dynamic equivalents between the issues that Jesus addressed in his day and those that our contemporary hearers face in our own time. This, it seems to me, is the essence of the evangelistic task. We bear witness to Jesus the *evangel* by allowing Him to draw attention to Himself in His own words.

Let me try to illustrate this line of thinking in very practical terms. For some years now, I have attempted to engage in this 'inside-out' style of apologetics by setting myself certain aims in answering the questions that non-Christians ask. I began to attempt to erase the 'I think. . . ' component of my responses of the 'outside-in' years and tried to start my replies along the lines of, 'It is interesting that you say that. . . *Jesus* was once asked a similar question and *He* said. . . ', or 'That's an interesting situation you describe. . . *Jesus* was once involved in a similar situation and *His* response was. . . ' The thrust of this approach can be illustrated by the diagram on the following page.

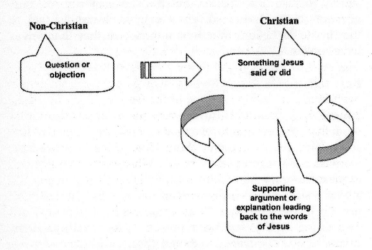

This approach seeks to bypass the more traditional 'bridging' material and cut straight to the chase. Of course – as the diagram illustrates – there is still often the need to engage in further apologetic argument, but the aim is not to let these secondary debates derail the evangelistic thrust. My aim at these points is to lead the discussion back to the words and teaching of Jesus.

It may be helpful at this stage to look briefly at some examples of this approach. First, I will look at two of the most common questions raised by non-believers in evangelistic conversations, and then comment on some of the wider themes that emerge from the gospels.

In practice – classic questions
Example 1: 'Isn't being good enough?'

The saving value of 'goodness' is a common theme in evangelistic dialogue: 'I try to help my neighbours and to do my best. No one can ask for more.' Or there is the parallel observation about sincerity, which runs along the lines: 'As long as you're sincere, I don't think it really matters what you believe.'

Using an 'outside-in' approach to this question, I would probably embark on a discussion about the relative standards of 'goodness', and how one might distinguish between them. By contrast, using an 'inside-out' approach, I will be asking myself whether Jesus was faced with a similar question, and if so how He answered it. I suggest in this context that John 6:27–29 is a very significant passage. Jesus is followed by crowds who have seen Him perform the miracle of the feeding of the five thousand. When they find Him, He warns them not to 'work for the food that perishes, but for the food that endures to eternal life'. Then John records that they asked Him: 'What must we do to perform the works of God?' (v. 28). What is required in God's sight to be acceptable to Him? Isn't this precisely the question about goodness posed by many of our contemporaries? Note then how Jesus answers. 'This is the work of God, that you believe in him whom he has sent' (v. 29). Jesus effectively refocuses the question from one about 'works' or 'goodness' to one about 'belief'. By doing so He cuts through the secondary questions and raises an intensely Christ-centred question.

So the reply to a contemporary questioner might run along the following lines: 'It's interesting that you raise the question of good deeds. Jesus was once asked a very similar question and He said that the work of God is to believe in the One He sent. In other words the first and most important thing we must "do" is to believe in the One whom God Himself sent into the world – Jesus Himself.' The conversation at this point will no doubt develop in one of a number of directions, but my experience is that it almost always raises the question of Jesus' identity, for what Jesus does constantly is to refocus the attention upon Himself, rather than upon other less important concerns.[17]

Example 2: 'Surely you cannot be saying that Jesus is the only way to God?'

The question about the uniqueness of Jesus will continue to be a central and provocative concern. It seems to most people extraordinary and unacceptable that Jesus is the *only* way by which people can be saved. Increasingly people will say something along the lines: 'I think in the end that all religions lead to God.'

But how do we answer this? With an 'outside-in' approach, my tendency was to use the phrase 'I think' – either to fudge the issue by saying that God will in the end do the just thing, or try to develop arguments that justify God's fairness in the Old Testament. Either way I found that hearers responded to *my* arguments about the defensibility of God's actions rather than to the gospel itself. By contrast, an 'inside-out' approach seeks once more to reply along the lines: 'It's interesting you should raise that question. Jesus himself said. . .' Where would we look? The most obvious place would be John 14:6–7. Here Jesus says, 'I am the way, and the truth, and the life. No one comes to the Father except through me. If you know me, you will know my Father also. From now on you do know him and have seen him.'

The most well-known part of this saying is the first clause. But for our purposes the more significant are the clauses that follow. Many postmoderns welcome the inclusiveness of Jesus, but baulk at His exclusiveness. In our text the inclusiv-ity of clause one is followed by the exclusivity of clause two, which in turn is explained by Jesus' reference to His identity in clause three. As before, our approach would seek to state Jesus' words explicitly as the response to the question raised by our listener. How the conversation would proceed would again vary, but as in the first example, the focus of the conversation invariably comes to revolve around the identity of Jesus Himself. The charge of arrogance levelled against the Christian position is not now aimed at the cleverness or content of my *own* arguments, but is directed at the seemingly unacceptable nature of the claims of Jesus.

The other side to the question about Jesus' exclusiveness is invariably what will happen to those who have never heard about Him. Once again, my own earlier approach had been to argue for the justice of God in quite abstract and complex terms. Latterly, however, I have used Jesus' words in Matthew 11:21–22: 'Woe to you, Chorazin! Woe to you, Bethsaida! For if the deeds of power done in you had been done in Tyre and

Sidon, they would have repented long ago in sackcloth and ashes.' At first sight this seems a strange saying to quote (especially to non-Christians), but its point is rather clear. What Jesus is saying in response to the unbelief He encounters in Galilee is that if similar things had been done in the cities of Tyre and Sidon, their inhabitants would have believed. In other words, Jesus knows the response they would have given to Him even when He had not gone there. The thrust of such words is the same as the more abstract argument about God's justice, except that it is much more succinct and focuses the hearer's attention back on to Jesus and His words.

In practice – contemporary themes

If the 'inside-out' approach can be applied to common questions and objections, it can also be used to address more general themes and issues. The key as before is to say something from the lips of Jesus about the kingdom in the context of the seemingly mundane and worldly. We have seen that this has two aspects: first, to make connections between the themes that arise at work or in home life and the issues that Jesus addresses; and second, to use Jesus' words to address them once again. Our evangelism training courses would be considerably enhanced (and far more productive) if we were to take the issues that have arisen in our own lives and those of our friends or colleagues and ask how Jesus addressed them.

Some of our answers to these questions will surprise us. Is it possible to retell the stories of Jesus to our friends? Yes, of course. At a pub meeting on a mission I was surprised when I heard myself relaying the story of the 'rich fool' in Luke 12 to a businessman with whom I had struck up a conversation about salaries. But why not? Isn't this precisely what evangelism is going to look like in a Christless society? If we take the opportunity to retell the gospel stories, and take the time to do so without apology, I fancy that we will be doing precisely what the earliest evangelists did. For the gospels were and are fundamentally evangelistic tools (see, for example, Mark 1:1; John 20:31). The best way to develop these skills is in company

with other Christians, taking perhaps a single issue each week
and asking what Jesus said about it – whether it be on the subject of money and wealth (for example Matthew 6:19–21, 19:23
[Mark 10:21–23; Luke 18:22–25]; Luke 6: 20,24, 12:15,16–21,
16:13,19–31), the vanity of pride (for example Matthew
20:26–28 [Mark 10:43–45]; Mark 7:20–23, 12:38–40; Luke
9:46–48, 18:10–14), or the origins and power of evil (for example Matthew 5:38–39; Mark 3:27, 7:20–23; John 12:31–32). Work
with these texts and try to tease out their relevance and application. You will find it a liberating discipline that will stretch
and excite your thinking about evangelism, as well as challenge the way you do it.

Three final thoughts

1. 'Pre'- and 'proper' evangelism

In the light of these observations the oft-quoted distinction
between the concepts of 'pre'-evangelism' and 'proper' evangelism appears to evaporate. If our method is to work from the
'inside' of the gospel, then there is no such thing as 'pre'-evan-
gelism. Take Mark's Gospel, for example, where the story of
Jesus' ministry begins with the shortest sermon on record:
'The Kingdom of God is at hand: repent and believe the good
news' (Mark 1:15). There is certainly nothing 'pre'- about this
statement. In one sense it sums up everything there is to say
about the kingdom. Everything else is an implication (or 'fall-
out') arising from this initial stupendous statement, involving
subsequent radical reorientation of both thought and action.[18]
Jesus *starts* therefore with a gospel announcement and works
through its implications in all that follows. It is interesting that
our contemporary strategies have tended to reverse this
process, starting with various 'bridging' or preparatory strategies designed to lead *towards* such an announcement.

2. 'Narrative' and truth

I mentioned earlier that the 'inside-out' approach helps to
meet the need for relational and conversational apologetics in

our contemporary postmodern setting. There are three aspects to this. First, at a pragmatic level, it enables a quicker engagement with the words and claims of Jesus than does a more reasoned, linear approach to apologetics. Second, at a communicational level, 'stories' and 'narratives' rather than abstract propositions and statements are more ideally suited to a postmodern mindset. People love to be told stories. They engage us and draw us in. In fact they are fundamental to our sense of identity because they give coherence and meaning to our lives. As Alasdair MacIntyre puts it, 'We all live out narratives in our lives and. . . we understand our own lives in terms of narratives that we live out.'[19] An apologetic strategy therefore that interconnects the daily narratives of our lives with *the* narrative of God's life – expressed in word and deed in the incarnation of Jesus – is ideally suited to a postmodern context.[20] Third, at a philosophical level, an 'inside-out' approach works by revealing the truth from 'within' the Christian 'narrative' rather than claiming prior philosophical truthfulness for that narrative from 'outside'. In other words, the claim that Jesus' words are true is one that authenticates itself in the process of explanation and investigation, rather than having to be authenticated by means of arguments about the reliability of the Bible.

3. Knowing the gospels

Finally, the experience of working at this style of evangelism is both exhilarating and demanding. But above all else it demands a much closer knowledge of the gospels than is commonly the case among Christians today. The philosopher Michael Polanyi used the term 'indwelling' to describe the type of knowledge we are aiming for. He used it to refer to that intimate kind of knowledge – like knowing how to ride a bike – that becomes second nature through being learnt.[21] By 'indwelling' such skills we are able to concentrate on further tasks (like navigation and taking in the view). In a parallel fashion we need to 'indwell' the gospel material so that it becomes part of our vocabulary, 'available' to us when we need it. When this is the case we can then concentrate on making 'connections'. In every experience of evangelism training along these lines, I have found that this is the single biggest issue. We simply don't know the gospels well enough.

So, although our contemporary setting poses great challenges to the Christian communicator, it is worth underlining the fact that postmodernity has not taken God by surprise! The rediscovery of the gospel narratives and their deployment in the work of evangelism seems to me to be one of the unused treasures of the Bible, which is especially appropriate in our day. May God grant us help in using them as they were originally used – for the sake of the kingdom. As John puts it: 'Jesus did many other signs in the presence of his disciples, which are not written in this book. But these are written so that you may come to believe that Jesus is the Messiah, the Son of God, and that through believing you may have life in his name' (John 20:30–31).

* * *

Revd Dr Paul Weston was formerly Vice-Principal of Oak Hill Theological College and is a member of the Church of England's 'College of Evangelists'.

Notes

1 E.R. Wickham, *Church and People in an Industrial City* (London: Lutterworth Press, 1957), p. 228.

2 London: Church House, 1991.

3 Ibid. pp. 3–4.

4 In the Anglican church the single largest group by percentage in 1979 was the under-fifteens. In 1998 it was the over-sixty-fives (Peter Brierley, *The Tide Is Running Out* [London: Christian Research, 2000]).

5 Quoted in Michael Riddell, *Threshold of the Future: Reforming the Church in the Post-Christian West* (London: SPCK, 1998), p. 101.

6 Terry Eagleton, 'Awakening from Modernity', *Times Literary Supplement*, 20 February 1987, p. 194.

7 Riddell, *Threshold of the Future*, p. 12.

8 Published respectively by The Navigators, Campus Crusade for Christ (now 'Agape') and St Matthias Press.

9 See C.H. Dodd, *The Apostolic Preaching and its Developments* (London: Hodder & Stoughton, 1936).

10 A good example of this is to be found in the summary material in John 3 following the interview with Nicodemus (John 3:16 ff.).

11 Compare e.g. Paul's sermon in Athens (Acts 17) with Peter's at Pentecost (Acts 2). Both are significant in specifically addressing questions raised by the hearers (cf. Acts 2:6–7, 2:12–13, 17:22–23). As a result of differing contexts (one conversant with the Old Testament, the other with Greek philosophy), the two sermons take differing shapes.

12 Walter Hollenweger, *Evangelism Today: Good News or Bone of Contention* (Belfast: Christian Journals, 1976), p. 81 (emphasis original).

13 John 3 is a classic example. Most commentators believe that verse 16 is the beginning of John's summary of Jesus teaching rather than a continuation of words actually spoken by Jesus. But in any case the summary statement (which continues to v. 21) can be seen to *follow* the evangelistic encounter rather than to precede it.

14 As a quick test, look at the content of the first session of your church's evangelistic 'Enquirers' course, and assess which approach it takes.

15 The statistics are quoted in J. Navone, 'The Dynamic of the Question in the Gospel Narratives', *Milltown Studies* 17 (1986). I am grateful to Dr Peter Head of Tyndale House, Cambridge for pointing out this article.

16 See e.g. Luke 10:36 for an example of the former and Mark 10:17–18 for the latter.

17 Other approaches to this question might use Jesus' conversation with the rich ruler with and the discussion about what real goodness is (Mark 10:17–27 and parallels). The sincerity question could be addressed in passages such as Matthew 7:21–23, 10:33, or John 14:6, where Jesus speaks about His exclusive and determinative role in relation to God. Consider also the stories of the two gates and the two builders (Matthew 7:3–14 and 7:24–27).

18 The Greek word for repentance, *metanoia*, literally means an 'after mind'.

19 Alasdair MacIntyre, *After Virtue: A Study in Moral Theory* (London: Duckworth, 1985²), p. 197.

20 It is striking in this context that Jesus often starts His dialogues with a comment, and then proceeds to tell a story to illustrate it (e.g. Luke 12:15, leading to vv. 16–21).

21 See Michael Polanyi, 'Faith and Reason', *Journal of Religion* 41 (1961), p. 242. Though Polanyi did not have Christian knowledge specifically in mind when he developed the term, Lesslie Newbigin applies Polanyi's thought to Christian concerns in many of his writings. See, for example, his *The Gospel in a Pluralist Society* (London: SPCK, 1989), pp. 98–9, 151, 232.